SPORTING LEGENDS OF IRELAND

TURTLE BUNBURY
AND JAMES FENNELL

MAINSTREAM
PUBLISHING

EDINBURGH AND LONDON

Copyright © text Turtle Bunbury, original portraits James Fennell, 2010
All rights reserved
The moral rights of the authors have been asserted

First published in Great Britain in 2010 by
MAINSTREAM PUBLISHING COMPANY (EDINBURGH) LTD
7 Albany Street
Edinburgh EH1 3UG

ISBN 9781845965020

A catalogue record for this book is available from the British Library

Typeset in Caslon, Requiem and Sabon

Printed in Great Britain by
Butler Tanner & Dennis Ltd, Frome, Somerset

ACKNOWLEDGEMENTS

This book is dedicated to our godchildren: Isabella Rose Nolan, Ted Johnson, Jessica Slingsby, Arthur Johnson, Alice Boyle, John Onions, Charlie Raben, Fonzy Ware, Bay Bunbury, Michaela Raben and Jack Rogers.

It is also for our perpetually beautiful wives, Ally and Jo, and for Lesley Fennell and Miriam Moore, without whom the creation of this book would not have been possible.

Sporting legends are always in demand. Every which way they look, another person is fast approaching, hoping they might sign an old jersey, star in a reality show, present a school prize, perform in a veterans' tournament, pose for a photograph, comment on a match, give a speech, patronise a charity.

As such, considerable assistance was required to make contact with the 44 legends in this book. We would especially like to thank Alan Sweetman, Jack Kyle, Dave Finlay Sr, Ronnie Delany, Mel Christle, Micheál Ó Muircheartaigh and Mathew Forde for taking the time to help us with our project and counsel us at the miscellaneous turns.

Thanks also to Graeme Blaikie and Claire Rose for their patient observations on matters mathematical and grammatical; to Ben and Jessica Rathdonnell for their kind assistance in proofreading; and to Ruth Cunney, who conceived of this project in the first place.

We would also like to thank the following:

Alan Aherne (Wexford People), Betty Ashe, Baltray Golf Club, Anne Marie Barnes, Ian Barrett, Jonah Barrington, Margaret Bennett, John Boomer, Brackencourt Hotel, Gill Browne, Averill Buchanan, Kevin Burke, Charlie Butler, Thomas Butler (Butler's Beans), Gerry Byrne, Des Cahill, Barry Chambers, Joe Christle, Ann Coghlan, Frank Columb, Terry Connaughton, Sam Cook, Tim Coote, Angus Craigie, Sue Craigie, Tom Crampton, Simon Cully, Chris Curran, Joe Curtis, Glenda Davies, Ger Delaney, Michael Delaney, Richard Denny, Simon Dick, Gay Dinan, Seamus Doherty, Louise Dolan, Mark Dorman, Niamh Doyle, Tamso Doyle, Brian Duggan, Cherri Dunlop, Thady and Geraldine Dunraven, Michael Edwards, Niamh Egan, Jim Fennelly, Alastair Fitch, Mary Foley (Wexford GAA), Michael Fortune, Allen Foster, Craig Foster, Charlie Fowler, Harry Fowler, Matthew Gallagher, Emma Galway, Trevor Gillespie, Des Gleeson, Thérèse Grogan, Alan Ryan Hall, Dennis Hanaghan, Camilla Haycock, Ted Hegarty, Emer Hynes, Elizabeth Igoe, the Irish Boxing Union, Robert Jebb, Hugo Jellett, Michael Johnston, Finbarr Kelleher, Jed and Lucy Kelly, Martin Kelly, Tomás Kelly (Rowing Ireland), Dermot Keogh, Joe Kirwan (the

Irish Amateur Boxing Association), John Kirwan, Niamh Kirwan, Gerard Lane, Emma Lane-Spollen, Michael Lanigan, John Laurinaitis, Ed Lindsay, James Lindsay-Finn, Zoe Lloyd, Pat Lynch, Charles Lysaght, Brion MacDomhnaill, Damhnaic Mac Eochaidh, Jamie Macken, Susanne Macken, Emily MacKenzie, Linda Madden, Clare Maguire, Niall Martin, Penny McBride, Mick McCloskey, Ian McClure, Alexisann McCrystal, Guy McCullough (Ballymena RFC), Michael McCumiskey, Pearl McDonald, Ann Marie McGing (Mayo County Council), Michael McGrath, Tom McGurk, David McHugh, Josie McKenna, Peter McKenna, Alex McKenzie, Alison McMahon, Deirdre McParland (Guinness Archive), Alan Milton, Aisling Moore, Maureen Mullins, Tony Mullins, Ger Murphy, Julie Newton, *The Sue Nunn Show*, Robert O'Byrne, Micheal O'Connell, Shane O Donohue, Susan O'Driscoll, Audrey O'Dwyer, Gillian O'Keefe, John O'Rawe (Belfast Bulls Wrestling Club), Colum O'Sullivan, Dawn Quinn (Irish Greyhound Board), Ned Quinn (Kilkenny County GAA), Mark Onions, Jeremy Perrin, Jason Popplewell, Michael Purcell, Michael Reidy, Eibhlin Roche (Guinness Archives), Roche Marina Hotel, Royal Co. Down Golf Club, Aileen Rogan (Tennis Ireland), Hannah Rowley, Steve Ryan, Fiona Sheridan (Royal Dublin Society), Laura Skelton (HorseSport Ireland), J.F. Steenhuis, Richard Street, Sinead Sunderland, Tom and Sasha Sykes, Mark Tottenham, Tara Tracey, Teresa Vahey, Conor Walsh, Dede Walsh, Denis Walsh, Shena Walsh, Ted Walsh, Sue Wickham, Marcus Williams, Tom Williams.

Should anyone have further historical information or anecdotes relating to sporting heroes or sporting venues that might have become neglected over the passage of time, they are advised to contact the website of the Irish Sporting Heritage Project.

Turtle Bunbury and James Fennell

CONTENTS

A SPORTING INTRODUCTION

What drives an individual to become dominant in any given sport? Is it down to their own sheer grit and determination? Is it simply instinctive? Or is it a case of incessant training making perfect? And, for that matter, is there a connection between sporting genius and geography or genetics?

Such were the questions pondered during interviews with forty-four of Ireland's foremost sporting icons over a six-month period. We have sought to create a book that is not simply about the GAA or rugby or horse racing but which embraces the broader spectrum of Irish sport as a whole, from wrestling and tennis to pole-vaulting and snooker.

The Tailteann Games, perhaps the oldest sporting event in history, are believed to have commenced in the second millennium BC and consisted of a 30-day festival on the banks of the River Blackwater in Co. Meath with gymnastic, equestrian and athletic events. One of the highlights was the chariot race, a sport that also took place on the Curragh in Celtic times, and which is indicative of Ireland's ancient fascination with the horse. During the medieval period, William Marshall, the original occupant of Kilkenny Castle, managed one of the finest jousting teams in Europe. Those same knights, many of whom lived in Ireland, were amongst the most fearsome fighters on the Crusades to the Middle East.

The sporting gene is evidently at its most ancient for those involved with horses. Charlie Swan's great-grandfather rode the winner of the 1863 Derby. Jessie Harrington, Willie Mullins and Ruby Walsh also belong to equestrian dynasties for whom the horse has been of central importance for as many generations as anyone can recall. Likewise, greyhound maestro Ger McKenna trained his greyhounds on the very same roads of Co. Tipperary along with his grandfather walked his back in the nineteenth century.

When one learns what someone's grandparents or parents did for a living, the reason why they fell into a particular sport often becomes apparent. World champion wrestler Dave Finlay Jr is the son and grandson of men who wrestled in Co. Antrim. World champion rower Niall O'Toole is the son and grandson of men who built boats for Guinness. Rally driver Rosemary Smith is the daughter of a garage owner. Eamonn Coghlan's father was an electrician who looked after the sound system at Croke Park.

It undoubtedly helps to have a sibling to compete against. Of the legends in this book, Packie Bonner, John Treacy and Angela Downey-Browne are twins, while Michael Carruth is a triplet. Jessie Harrington and June Ann Fitzpatrick competed for Ireland alongside their brothers. Des Smyth played golf with his brothers. Ronnie Delany ran alongside his, as did Mary Peters. Willie Mullins rode out with his, while Niall O'Toole was determined to out-row his. Likewise, Stephen Roche's son Nicolas is now one of Europe's leading cyclists, while Ducksie Walsh's son Dylan was the 2010 Under-15s champion at the US Handball Association championships.

But a surprising number of legends are one-offs, the first of their family to make a go of it in the sporting world. Willie John McBride, Cora Staunton, Eddie Macken, Sonia O'Sullivan, Jack O'Shea, Maeve Kyle, Conor O'Dwyer – all simply took a liking to their chosen sport by dint of personal taste and circumstance.

During the age of Empire, the British developed the idea of team sports where groups of, say, 11 or 15 men were effectively given a ball and instructed to work as one unit, mastering trust, communication, leadership, responsibility and suchlike. Team sports were particularly well suited to the British military ethos and it is no coincidence that many of Ireland's garrison towns became strongholds for such games. Kilkenny, Tipperary, Cork and Carlow were epicentres for cricket. Sligo and Donegal developed as soccer Meccas. Rugby also took hold in pockets across the country with a high density of soldiers or gentry.

Golf became a sport of choice for the well-to-do, and the Irish coast is exceptionally well suited to links golf, combining great beauty with the ideal sands and rugged terrain. Tennis also developed into a hugely popular game amongst the upper classes, and during the 1890s and early twentieth century Ireland's tennis elite racked up nine Wimbledon titles, as well as two Olympic golds, the Australian Open, the US Open and, effectively, the Davis Cup.

It is hard to think of another country that has politicised sport to the same degree as Ireland. South Africa under apartheid probably comes closest. During the late nineteenth century, many landed estates in Ireland were able to field teams for both hurling and cricket matches. Several of those who played in the first All-Ireland hurling final were considered excellent cricket players. However, the Gaelic Athletic Association's ban on any of its members playing 'garrison games' or 'foreign sports' was one of the defining aspects of Anglo-Irish relations for much of the twentieth century.

Likewise, few events symbolised just how awful the fight for independence was than the Sunday afternoon in November 1920 when British guns opened fire on the players and crowd gathered for a Gaelic football match in Croke Park. It is to the great credit of the Irish people that they accepted that the crushing defeat inflicted on the English rugby team at Croke Park in 2007 was a fitting time to conclude the horror of that first Bloody Sunday.

Away from politics, the GAA has achieved an enormous amount in re-establishing indigenous Gaelic games across Ireland, albeit with new and ever-changing rules. Gaelic football, for instance, evolved from an inter-parish 'free-for-all', without rules or even a defined playing area or time limit. It is also notable how influential geography is in terms of a sport such as Gaelic football. Take Co. Kerry, where everybody lives for the game and no conversation is complete without mention of Mick O'Dwyer, Mick O'Connell or Jack O'Shea. That fervent passion is undoubtedly why Co. Kerry, with its population of *circa* 160,000 people, has utterly dominated the All-Ireland football championships, winning the title on 36 occasions.

The last time Co. Kerry's hurlers won the All-Ireland was in 1891. Conversely, Co. Kilkenny remains defiantly at the very bottom of the Gaelic football league. But give them a stick, and the men and women of Kilkenny are likely to run away with the show. The county has won 32 All-Ireland hurling titles, with Eddie Keher and D.J. Carey to the fore, while Angela Downey-Browne helped Kilkenny win 12 All-Ireland camogie championships.

Northern Ireland continues to confuse the international circuit in terms of its sporting identity. Many of its athletes represent Great Britain at the Olympics, its rugby players wear the green jerseys of Ireland and its soccer players perform proudly under the flag of Northern Ireland itself. To delicately leapfrog such issues, we have included in this volume seven Northern Irish sporting legends of miscellaneous disciplines.

On the international stage Ireland has had a staggeringly successful sporting record, not least considering our population is the same size as Birmingham's. Nine of Ireland's twenty Olympic medals have been won by boxers. That surely says something about the Irish mindset and how we seem to relish the prospect of being the underdog and having to fight harder. Certainly, the legends in this book are resilient souls. Mick O'Dwyer broke both his legs in 1964 and continued to play football for the next three decades. Stephen Martin was told he would never play sport again and went on to win an Olympic gold medal. Barry McGuigan nearly retired from boxing when he fatally injured another man in the ring; he stayed on and became world featherweight champion. Rosemary Smith thought she would never drive again when her navigator went crashing through the windscreen of their rally car; she went on to become the greatest lady driver of her day.

Many legends are remarkably versatile, enabling them to excel at several sports at once. As a handballer, hurler D.J. Carey has won three All-Irelands and two world titles. Willie John McBride started as a pole-vaulter before moving to rugby. Steve Collins has swapped the boxing ring for the hunt. Mary Sinnott-Dinan was considered one of the greatest camogie players ever when she switched to badminton. Poker champion Donnacha O'Dea was the first Irishman to swim 100 m in less than a minute.

Whether or not Gaelic games ultimately go down the road to professionalism, it remains imperative that the development of sporting infrastructure at local level continues across Ireland for all sports. Indeed, if the right infrastructure is in place, there is a very good chance that people from that locality will excel. Handball is a case in point. The Countess of Desart built a handball club in Kilkenny City a century ago; the club has since won more than 100 All-Ireland senior medals, including 38 for Ducksie Walsh. Over in Newport, Co. Mayo, Charlie McGee constructed a rather more modest handball court; his son Peadar went on to win 18 national medals. Down in the Wexford village of Taghmon, they ensured the court came complete with badminton lines; Mary Sinnott of that village won eight All-Ireland badminton titles. The story is echoed in other sports. Des Smyth grew up beside a golf course, Jack O'Shea beside a football pitch, Alan Lewis beside a cricket club.

There is, of course, a difference between those who play sport at professional level and those who remain amateurs. Most sports have now become professional, as Sky Sports and suchlike seek to reap the financial benefits. The amateur sportsman retains a considerable charm. Willie John McBride, the rugby lock who worked as a banker in Belfast. Peter Canavan, the footballer who teaches PE at a school in Cookstown. Denny Hyland, the pole-vaulter who made hydraulics in Carlow. Michael Carruth, the boxer who marched out with the Irish army. By and large, all of these legends played their games, celebrated or commiserated accordingly that night, and then returned to their day jobs.

But for many, when the option came to turn pro, they accepted it, be they athletes like Sonia O'Sullivan and Ronnie Delany, who were offered a place at the great sporting universities of the USA, or snooker players like Ken Doherty. And it must be some compensation for jockeys like Ruby Walsh to at least know that he is being paid every time he is catapulted from the saddle towards another broken rib. The same cannot be said for GAA players such as ladies' footballer Cora Staunton, who, now 28, expects to be fully arthritic by her early 40s.

Much about sport changes, just as everything becomes more physical and professional. It's not quite such an affordable pastime as it once was. Shoes are cushier. Games are shorter. Stoppages are more frequent. You're allowed to rehydrate yourself. The ball is more predictable. Fifty years ago, for instance, a football absorbed the weather conditions on the pitch so that if it was raining, the water and mud would seep in and the ball would get heavier by the minute. Rules are also ever evolving, as international rugby and GAA players alike discovered in 2010. Even something as time-honoured as horse racing is facing change, not least since the identification of the so-called 'speed genes' possessed by every winning thoroughbred.

But while some things change, our need for heroes remains. If Louk Sorensen won Wimbledon, no tennis court in Ireland would be empty. When Jack Charlton's army ran rampant in the World Cup campaigns of 1990 and 1994, every schoolboy in the country took a fancy for soccer. The ongoing golden age of Irish rugby has seen youngsters from all four provinces turn with a passion to the game with the curiously shaped ball. Golf too is now hugely attractive to many younger players, with Padraig Harrington, Graeme McDowell and Rory McIlroy dominating the global elite. Cricket has also enjoyed a renaissance ever since Ireland's cricketers defeated Pakistan in the 2007 World Cup. And, of course, the fervour of the annual All-Ireland football, hurling and camogie championships continue to excite the island on a regular basis.

The reason why the people in this book are deemed legends is that they are pioneers of their game, people who have converted their zeal and stamina into victory, men and women who had the commitment and the will to win, trailblazers who challenged things and raised the bar for everyone else. For some it involved endless practice. For others it was sheer instinct. All are legends and to them we bow.

Turtle Bunbury

Sporting Legends
of Ireland

D.J. CAREY

Hurling and Handball

Hurling

TITLES
All-Ireland: 5
Leinster: 10
National League: 4

AWARDS
All Stars: 9
Texaco Hurler of the Year, 1993, 2000
Eircell Hurler of the Year, 2000
Kilkenny Hurling Team of the Century, 1999

Handball

TITLES
All-Ireland Doubles: 3
World Championships 23 and Under
  Singles and Doubles

'I've broken my nose three or four times,' says Kilkenny hurler D.J. Carey. 'I've had over 250 stitches to my face and head. You expect that. Many players break a hand or a finger or a wrist in the game and just play on. When the blood's up, you don't notice. It's when you cool down that the real pain comes.'

The Beatles performed live together more than 1,200 times before 'I Want to Hold Your Hand' broke into America. It's said that Mozart played on the piano for some 10,000 hours before he produced his first masterwork. And D.J. Carey must have slammed the sliotar into the wall of his parents' house 100,000 times before he secured his debut on Kilkenny's victorious All-Ireland minor team back in 1988. That year was the start of a most beautiful friendship between D.J. and the Kilkenny Cats.

Without doubt, D.J. has been Ireland's most influential hurler of the past two decades. Using what Tom Humphries called 'the burst of pace of a scalded cat', he scored 34 goals and 195 points in 57 championship games. By 2002, he had amassed nine All Stars (an achievement matched only by Kerry's Pat Spillane and Carey's Kilkenny heir, Henry Shefflin), and he is among the five top-scoring hurlers in history. He has appeared for Kilkenny more often than anyone else and, on the side, he happens to be a two-time world handball champion.

The Carey family originally hailed from Galmoy, a small village on the broad plains of north-east Kilkenny, well known for its lead and zinc mines. D.J.'s grandfather John Carey was born on a small farm just outside the village in 1899. The zest for the hurl came into the family in the late 1930s, when John married Catherine Phelan, a sister of legendary hurler Paddy Phelan, a winner of four All-Ireland medals. Paddy's passion inspired John and Catherine's daughter Peggy to take up the stick and so D.J.'s aunt went on to scoop four All-Ireland camogie titles with Kilkenny in the 1970s.

In 1956, John Carey sold the land at Galmoy and relocated to Gowran, Co. Kilkenny, where he set up a cattle farm. In time, the farm passed to his son, also John, who married Maura McGarry of Kilkenny City. Born in St Luke's Hospital, Kilkenny, in November 1970, Denis Joseph Carey was the eldest of their seven children.

D.J. believes that at least some of his success was determined by geography. Young boys in Kilkenny generally know how to catch a sliotar on a hurl long before they've mastered the toothbrush. D.J. was a toddler when he gripped his first hurl. Fuelling that clench was the success of Kilkenny's hurlers, who won five All-Ireland titles before his thirteenth birthday.

'I played for Kilkenny at a time when that team was on a roll. That gave me a high profile. But if I had been born five miles away in Co. Carlow, then maybe I'd have played for Carlow instead. Carlow may be going well these days, but I could have played for them for 18 years and maybe we would never have got past the first round of a championship.'

Given that his aunt Peggy and great-uncle Paddy won eight All-Irelands between them, one could be forgiven for thinking that sporting prowess is genetic. D.J. doesn't buy into that. 'By God, you have to work at these things,' he says. 'It wasn't something handed down to me and all of a sudden I was good. I became good because I wore out a wall when I was young, hitting the ball off it, practising all day, every day. There's also the fact that I wanted to be my hero, Eddie Keher, and so every time I hit that spot on the wall, I was pretending to be Eddie scoring a point or a goal.' The nearby window was apparently broken so many times his mother gave up replacing it.

By the early 1980s, he was one of the leading lights of Gowran's Young Ireland hurlers. He honed his skills at St Kieran's College in Kilkenny, a celebrated hotbed of hurling talent where his mother Maura worked, winning consecutive All-Ireland colleges titles in 1988 and 1989. In the latter year, he played for both Kilkenny's minor and senior teams, respectively winning the All-Ireland and the league.

In 1992, the twenty-one year old slammed a crucial goal into the net to help Kilkenny win its first All-Ireland seniors title in nine years. D.J. was to be an indispensable part of the team for the next 12 years, during which time hurling evolved into a much more physically demanding game. One of his most sublime performances was during the 1997 All-Ireland quarter-final, in which he almost single-handedly annihilated Galway.

D.J., one of the sport's gentlemen, is a serious man. 'But there is great fun in the dressing room after a match,' he promises. 'Maybe a couple of funny guys or a couple of stupid guys acting funny. Some of the undergarments the guys wore at times . . . when I started, the togs were up around your hips and crotch. That was the great fashion. Now it's nearly around your ankles and there's guys wearing socks above their knees.'

The camaraderie appealed to him, particularly in club hurling. 'When myself and Charlie Carter and a few others were getting older – and getting older together – and we obviously weren't as fast and as fit as we once were, we'd sometimes be inclined to let someone else go for the ball instead. There is always a bit of humour from your own side then, no doubt about it.'

D.J.'s attempt to retire gracefully in 1998 was thwarted when the postman delivered some 25,000 letters urging him to stay at his post. He went on to become one of the most electric linchpins (and sometimes captain) of Brian Cody's record-breaking Cats, winning three All-Ireland titles and two league titles in the first five years of the present century. No Kilkenny match was complete without a considerable percentage of the crowd chanting 'D.J.! D.J.! D.J.!' over and over again, willing him to score one of his trademark late goals.

His final appearance in the black and amber stripes was in the 2005 All-Ireland semi-final, when Kilkenny fell to Galway. He retired at the start of the 2006 championship to concentrate on charity work, his golfing handicap and his hygiene business, D.J. Carey Enterprises, which sees him clocking up approximately 80,000 km a year in Ireland. He is also regularly to be found presenting medals at schools and clubs. D.J. is separated from his wife, with whom he has two children, and lives with Essex-born dot-com entrepreneur Sarah Newman, well-known for her role in the Irish version of *Dragons' Den*.

Clad in the colours of his home club, Young Ireland, D.J. Carey prepares to strike out in the 2004 Kilkenny senior hurling final. D.J. joined the Gowran-based club in 1988 and remained with them until 2007, during which time he also became the powerhouse of the Kilkenny county team.
(© Pat Murphy/Sportsfile)

EDDIE KEHER

Hurling

TITLES
All-Ireland: 6
Leinster: 10
National League: 3

AWARDS
Cú Chulainn: 4
All Stars: 5
Texaco Hurler of the Year, 1972
GAA Hurling Team of the Century, 1984
GAA Hurling Team of the Millennium, 1999
RTÉ/Irish Sports Council Hall of Fame, 2003
Texaco Hall of Fame, 2009

Location certainly has a lot to do with it. D.J. Carey reckons that if he had been born five miles east, he would have been classed as a Carlow man and would thus have been unlikely to pursue his passion for hurling to any great depth. Likewise the fate of D.J.'s childhood hero Eddie Keher was dictated when his father, then a young garda, was transferred from his native Roscommon to Co. Kilkenny in 1932.

Eddie would go on to become arguably the greatest hurler of the twentieth century, helping Kilkenny win six All-Irelands and ten Leinster titles in a remarkable eighteen-year inter-county career between 1959 and 1977. For 38 years, Eddie was hurling's all-time greatest championship marksman. His tally of 36 goals and 337 points in 50 games was considered virtually untouchable. And then, in June 2010, another extraordinary Kilkenny forward, Henry Shefflin, relieved him of that honour. But Henry Shefflin's story is for another day.

The Eddie Keher story begins in the rolling countryside due west of Roscommon Town, where his grandfather Peter Keher tended a flock of sheep in the lush pastures that surround Donamon Castle on the banks of the salmon-rich River Suck. In 1884, the year the GAA was founded, the 21-year-old shepherd was married. His wife, Ellen, bore him nine children, six of whom survived to adulthood. Amongst these was Eddie's father, Stephen Keher, who was born in 1898.

During the 1920s, Stephen and his brothers hurled for the local Donamon club. However, Stephen liked football better and played on the Roscommon senior football team on a few occasions. Indeed, despite his son's success, Stephen always preferred football to hurling.

In 1932, Donamon Castle was taken over by the Irish Republican Army and converted into a training ground. By then, Stephen Keher had joined the Garda Síochána and, that

same year, he was transferred to Kilkenny District where he served in Kilkenny City, Tullaroan and Inistioge, a pretty tree-lined village that sprawls through the Nore Valley.

Inistioge was to be the setting for the romance between the young garda from Roscommon and his bride to be, Noreen Browne. They were wed in 1935. Their second child, Eddie, was born on 14 October 1941.

From the age of eight, the boy showed himself to be a hurler of note, battling it out in evening matches played between Inistioge's 'up streets' and 'down streets', or between lads from the village and the surrounding country. In July 1952, the 11 year old played for Inistioge when they won the Under-14 Roinn B hurling county final. They won again in 1955 and that time Eddie Keher was Man of the Match.

For many decades, St Kieran's College in Kilkenny has been considered Ireland's foremost hurling nursery. Its past pupils include Brian Cody, D.J. Carey, Henry Shefflin, Eoin and Philly Larkin and James 'Cha' Fitzpatrick. But none has had a greater impact on the sport than Eddie, who began his secondary education there in 1954.

Perhaps the greatest influence in Eddie's life was Father Tommy Maher, who became a teacher at St Kieran's in 1955. A remarkable hurler in his own right, Father Maher coached St Kieran's to a series of victories in both the junior and senior Leinster colleges championships. Eddie was the star player in both teams.

In 1957, he struck home three second-half goals to help St Kieran's win the All-Ireland senior colleges final. Two years later, the 17 year old captained St Kieran's to win his second All-Ireland title.

In 1956, he was called up to play for the Kilkenny minors, with whom he won four Leinster medals, losing to Tipperary in the All-Ireland finals of 1956 and 1959, and to Galway in the 1958 semi-final.

Although the Cats were beaten, Eddie's performance against Tipperary in the 1959 minor final impressed the Kilkenny selectors so much that he was summoned again for the county in the All-Ireland senior final replay against Waterford. Kilkenny fell again but it was noted that the two meagre points they scored in the second half both came from the stick of the young corner-forward from Inistioge. Eddie remains the only man to have appeared in senior and minor finals in the same year.

After St Kieran's, he went to Rosse College in Dublin, trained in banking and began working for the Allied Irish Bank at their Dublin branches on St Stephen's Green and Capel Street. The 1960s had begun and Eddie was about to become the most famous bank official in the Republic.

In 1962, he was on the Kilkenny team when they won their first league title since 1933. In 1963, people from all across the nation tuned in to Telefís Éireann and watched Eddie play an out-and-out blinder in the All-Ireland final, skipping through the Waterford defence to smash home a record 14 points and ensure Kilkenny finished up champions.

Eddie's triumphant performance was no fluke. Like D.J. Carey a generation later, he achieved his excellence by practice. The evening before every game he played, he was out in the field in Inistioge, hitting the ball, perfecting his method long into the night. 'I kept experimenting for hours on end,' he says, 'until I evolved a system of rising and hitting the ball that I knew must succeed.' And succeed it did, as Kilkenny won the All-Ireland in 1967, 1969 (with Keher as captain), 1972, 1974 and 1975.

In the summer of 1972, Eddie met Muhammad Ali in Enniskerry, Co. Wicklow, and taught

the heavyweight champion how to hurl. 'He was a hero of mine,' says Eddie, 'but I was surprised by how quiet he was . . . until we met with the press.' Eddie's father Stephen had been a passionate boxing fan for a long time and was fascinated by Ali. 'I still remember getting up in the middle of the night to listen to the Ali–Sonny Liston bout with him on the radio.' Eddie took his father to see Ali fight Al Lewis later in the week. It wasn't a great match, but the Kehers enjoyed it. 'When Ali went in for the kill, there was no stopping him,' Eddie recalls.

Two months later, Eddie's career-defining moment came during the All-Ireland final against Cork. With less than twenty minutes to go before the full-time whistle, the Leesiders were leading by eight points. All seemed lost until, almost out of nowhere, Eddie was spotted leaping into the sky, grabbing the sliotar and sprinting up the sideline. As he pucked the sliotar, it looked like it was looping upwards for a certain point. Then it stalled just short of the bar and, as if redirected by the gods, shot past the startled Cork goalkeeper into the back of the net. It provided the impetus for one of the greatest turnarounds in All-Ireland-final history.

Eddie retired from hurling in 1977 to concentrate on his banking career and his golf (he's a nine-handicapper). In 1987, he became manager of the Allied Irish Bank in Callan, Co. Kilkenny. In 1979, he and fellow former player Pat Henderson joined forces to manage Kilkenny and, once again, the Cats lifted the All-Ireland trophy. Eddie had less success coaching Kilkenny single-handedly for a season in 1987, when the team were ousted from the championship early on.

In 1978, Eddie teamed up with Father Tommy Murphy and Garda Éamonn Doyle to found the No Name Club in Kilkenny. The club aimed to tackle Ireland's spiralling drink and drugs situation by providing young people with credible alternatives to pub culture. The club now has more than 40 branches nationwide and upwards of 15,000 members.

In the summer of 1969, Eddie Keher captained Co. Kilkenny to annihilate London Exiles in the All-Ireland senior hurling semi-final at Croke Park. Kilkenny went on to win the Liam McCarthy Cup as Eddie claimed the third of his six All-Ireland championships. (© Connolly Collection/Sportsfile)

MICK O'CONNELL

Gaelic Football

TITLES
All-Ireland: 4
Munster: 12
National League: 6

AWARDS
All Stars: 1
Texaco Footballer of the Year, 1962
GAA Football Team of the Century, 1984
GAA Football Team of the Millennium, 2000
RTÉ/Irish Sports Council Hall of Fame, 2002

Some islands are more discreet than others. The now deserted Beginis Island, for instance, has been sitting quietly on the big toe of Kerry's Iveragh Peninsula since the world was young. And yet very few of those who have tootled around the Ring of Kerry in past decades would know its name. The larger island to the west? Yes, no problem. That's Valentia Island, the one that sounds Spanish and from where they ran the telegraph cable all the way across the Atlantic to Newfoundland back in 1866. But Beginis?

The Vikings knew about Beginis. Scattered relics from their kitchens and farmsteads have survived the storms of a thousand years. By the nineteenth century, the southern shores of the island were home to a handful of cattle-farming families, none feistier than the O'Connells.

Jeremiah O'Connell, Mick's father, was born on the island in 1894. During the 1920s and '30s, there was a concentrated effort by the Irish government to move people off such isolated islands. In 1935, Jeremiah and his wife, Mary (who came from the Kerry mainland), moved from Beginis to Valentia, where Jeremiah continued to work as a fisherman, farmer and ship's pilot.

His son Mick, or Micko, was born on Valentia two years later. He lived the outdoors life from the outset, working in the fields with his father and brothers, rowing to secondary school in Cahersiveen. 'In a way, we were self-sufficient, and we had a decent life,' he recalls. 'The island was idyllic and it was a lovely place to grow up.' When a storm, a big

tide and a full moon coincide, Mick reckons, the roar from the ocean is louder than Croke Park can ever be.

South Kerry has long been a footballing stronghold. During Mick's childhood, Valentia's footballers – known as the 'Young Islanders' – won the South Kerry title three times. Mick and his school pals scampered out to the fields with their gnarly old footballs and sought to emulate their heroes. Mick impressed from an early age. Back at home, he would kick a ball against the gable end of his family's two-storey house, using both feet, thundering the ball with all his might and then leaping and twisting to catch it on the return, always conscious of the angle and the height.

In 1957, Mick O'Connell played centre-field for the Young Islanders when they overcame strong favourites Renard to reclaim the South Kerry championship. His presence on the Valentia team ignited a golden age for the club, and between 1957 and 1964 they won seven South Kerry senior championships.

Meanwhile, his county record wasn't looking so bad either. He made his debut for Kerry in the 1955 Munster minor championship. The following year, he lined out for the Kerry seniors. In 1958, he helped the Kingdom win the first of eight consecutive Munster titles. In 1959, aged 22, he captained the green and gold to victory in both the National Football League and the All-Ireland senior final. The islander had very quickly become a household name.

No doubt on account of his island roots, Mick is a unique individual. While the rest of Kerry celebrated the 1959 triumph long into the night, Mick caught a train back home from Dublin so he could be at work next morning. 'I was working with the cable company and all the others were going to be there, so why should I get excused because of my sport? Medals or trophies were never important to me. I only collected the cup because it was my duty to do so.' There was no mention of the knee he twisted during the game.

Mick's brilliance was almost certainly down to his gruelling, if unconventional, fitness regime. 'Ninety per cent of my training exercises were done at home and on my own,' he says. He famously rowed to and from Valentia before and after matches. Rowing remains his preferred mode of transport and he still frequently rows from the island to the Kerry mainland. The exercise gave him arguably the most powerful shoulders in GAA history and an upper body to match. When not rowing, he was constantly running, heaving, pushing, lifting, jumping, always looking to break a sweat. 'Training was an obsession with me,' he readily admits. 'Every day was geared to it.'

Mick's finest game was probably the final of the 1961 National League, when Kerry hammered Derry 4–16 to 1–5 in Croke Park. The late John D. Hickey, the greatest sportswriter of the day, described Mick as 'a football sorcerer . . . who must unquestionably rank as the best midfielder the game has known'.

As fellow footballer Paul Russell put it, 'He controls [the ball] and uses it as if there was a magnet on his hands and feet. His every move has exquisite grace and poetic rhythm. All his actions are the outward magnifications of a razor-keen football mind.'

Mick O'Connell remained the dominant – and most elegant – player in the midfield throughout the 1960s. In 1969, he won his fourth National League medal, his tenth Munster title and his third All-Ireland medal. The following year, he began his third decade of inter-county football by helping Kerry defeat Meath in the first 80-minute All-Ireland final. By the time he retired in 1973, Mick had played in nine All-Ireland football finals and won four. He also helped Kerry win six National League medals between 1959 and 1972.

Mick played in an age when high catches and long, accurate kicks were every bit as important as speed, fitness and hand-passing. He is famously reserved in his enthusiasm for the modern game. 'It's more like basketball than the old traditional catch-and-kick. It's a throw-ball game. The skill is gone out of it, for me. It's win at any cost and I don't like it.'

Mick lives on Valentia with his wife, Rosaleen. They have two sons and a daughter. Their younger son, Diarmuid, has Down's syndrome and also lives on the island. 'I can honestly say he is the greatest gift I was ever given,' says Mick. 'He has brought untold joy into our lives and we love him dearly. My wife is deeply involved with raising funds for the handicapped and I support her as much as I can.'

Co. Kerry's Mick O'Connell (centre) soars for a high ball in the 1968 All-Ireland senior football final, out-jumping Co. Down's Sean O'Neill (left) and John Purdy. Kerry ultimately lost the match but, with 'Micko' on the team, they bounced back to reclaim the championship in 1969.
(© Connolly Collection/Sportsfile)

MICK O'DWYER

Gaelic Football

TITLES

As Player
All-Ireland: 4
Munster: 12
National League: 8

As Manager
All-Ireland: 8
Munster: 13
National League: 3

AWARDS

GAA Football Top Scorer, 1960, 1970
Texaco Footballer of the Year, 1969
Philips Sports Manager of the Year, 1984
Texaco Hall of Fame, 2004
RTÉ/Irish Sports Council Hall of Fame, 2009

Mick O'Dwyer reins his BMW up in Baltinglass Square, Co. Wicklow, and throws me a wave. I'm standing beside a monument to the 1798 rebel hero Michael Dwyer. 'My father's people had a farm about three miles south of Waterville, Co. Kerry,' says Mick, looking up at the statue. 'His name was John and his father's name was Michael, known as Mick, but it would be a stretch to make them related to this man.'

Mick has just driven direct from the Atlantic-scented streets of Waterville and is on his way to Roundwood, up in the Wicklow Mountains to the north. It's an average enough journey for the 73-year-old footballing legend, who generally racks up 70,000 miles a year. But sitting in the car has certainly not slowed him down and soon we are pacing around Baltinglass Golf Club, of which he is a member.

'My mother was the oldest of seventeen and my father was one of fifteen,' he says, acknowledging the salutations of passers-by. Mick is an exceptionally well-known figure in Ireland. And rightly so. As player and manager, he has won more than half of the 21 All-Ireland senior football finals he has been directly involved in since 1959.

'My mother's people,' he continues, 'were fishermen and small farmers from Scariff Island, just off the west coast. Her name was Mary Galvin and she was the last of the family to be born on the island. It was tough but it was very healthy. They weren't worried about making millions or billions. They were quite happy to exist and enjoy their

life. It was wonderful the way the people rambled around to each other's houses every other night for chats and to play cards and all that. Then we got the satellite telly in and that destroyed it. Now when you go into the houses, the first thing they say is "shush", because they're watching *Coronation Street*. That's technology for you.'

Shortly after Mary's birth, the Galvins 'came ashore and moved to a most beautiful place called Bunavalla', close to Derrynane Harbour, where Mick spent many childhood summers.

John O'Dwyer, Mick's father, was a sheep farmer who favoured the hunting, shooting, fishing style of life, maintaining a small pack of beagle hounds. 'We'd be out with the foot hounds every Sunday and Wednesday, from October to March, all day long,' says Mick.

Long before he turned his hand to management, Mick O'Dwyer was one of the stalwarts of Co. Kerry's football team, winning four All-Ireland medals and eleven Munster titles, including six in a row from 1958 to 1963. (© Connolly Collection/Sportsfile)

One way or another, John took a shine to Mary Galvin, who was head cook at the Butler Arms Hotel at Waterville for close on 35 years, during the days when Charlie Chaplin was a frequent visitor. John and Mary fell in love and were wed. With 30 siblings between them, they opted for a small family. 'Just the one between them,' laughs Mick. 'I'm an only child.'

Mick's father was great on the fiddle and accordion, but he 'hadn't too much interest in Gaelic football'. The footballing came from his mother's side. Five of her brothers played for Derrynane and some also played for South Kerry.

But Mick credits his passion for the sport to John McCarthy, his primary-school teacher in Waterville, who did much to organise games between schools in the area during his childhood. 'He had a baby Ford and he'd put the whole team in it, 14 or 15 of us,' he marvels.

When he left school, Mick became a mechanic and focused his ambitions on being a rally driver. However, his football prowess was becoming apparent and his father encouraged him, insisting that there could be no finer honour than to wear the green and gold. In 1954, a local garda drove him 50 miles north to Tralee for his first trial with the Kerry minors. He duly became the first player from Waterville to wear a Kerry jersey in any grade. Most of Waterville made their way to Kenmare to watch him score 1–7 against Waterford in the Munster semi-final. But in those days, the 'remote' players of south Kerry were often relegated, and young 'Micko' was on the bench for the Munster final, which Kerry won.

He began playing for the seniors in 1956 and made his first appearance in a championship match in 1957. Two years later, he was on the Kerry team that won both the National League and the All-Ireland. Over the next fourteen years, Mick would gather a trophy chest of four All-Ireland, eight league and twelve Munster titles. This was despite his 1965 horror when he broke both his legs, only to bounce back and play a starring role in the 1968 campaign.

In 1974, Mick retired as a player and the following year he became Kerry manager. That summer, he took his team north to take on Kevin Heffernan's Dublin, then the strongest team in Ireland. Kerry stunned the Dubs with a seven-point win and an exciting and intense new rivalry between Kerry and Dublin broke upon the country.

Mick is famous for his old-school training – wire-to-wire runs and endless laps – holding that there's no finer way to watch a player's fitness improving. He once took the Kerry team out training 27 nights in a row. As Jack O'Shea has put it, 'He was always one of us but we still listened to what he said like he was a god.' And he sure gets the results. During his twelve years as manager, Mick took his team to ten All-Ireland finals and won eight of them. In 1986, he was named Kerryman of the Year.

He continued to play inter-county for Waterville until he was 37 and remained on the pitch at his club until he was accidentally kicked in the head and suffered a serious injury at the age of 48.

During the 1990s, he single-handedly revived Gaelic football in Co. Kildare, managing the Lilywhites to a Leinster title and the All-Ireland final. In 2003, he nearly did the same again for Co. Laois, taking them, via a Leinster title, to the quarter-finals. More recently, as manager of Co. Wicklow, he led the Garden County to victory in the 2007 Tommy Murphy Cup.

He is also a man of keen business acumen. In 2005, he chose the perfect time to sell his pub in Newbridge and one of his two hotels. He now owns a series of fast-food restaurants, rather controversially insisting that if only people exercised, it would not matter what they ate. Mick can operate grand on five hours' sleep, so long as he gets a forty-minute walk every day, and plenty of golf, to keep him in shape. He plays the button accordion when he can and likes to fish around the islands where his ancestors lived. 'It's great to get out on the sea and away from it all.'

'I had a wonderful time through football,' he says. 'It took me all over the world. I even went to a place called Wagga Wagga in Australia, if you ever heard tell of it? And, yes, it is still all go. But why should I take it slow? There's only one thing for life: keep going as long as you can. Any man who thinks about retiring, you might as well get the coffin.' And then, a smile spreading, 'I do be doing undertaking as well, you see!'

JACK O'SHEA

Gaelic Football

TITLES
All-Ireland: 7
Munster: 10
National League: 3

AWARDS
All Stars: 6
Texaco Footballer of the Year, 1980, 1981, 1984, 1985
GAA Football Team of the Century, 1984

'We didn't have a television in our house,' says Jack O'Shea. 'We rented one for a week at Christmas and that was it. So we got up to all the devilment we could outside, having hunts and chasing each other after school. Everything revolved around exercise. We didn't have a car, either, so if we had to go to our grandmother or uncle, we'd cycle six or seven miles from our house.'

Jack's house was on New Street in Cahersiveen, the village on the western edge of Kerry's Iveragh Peninsula where the legendary footballer was born in November 1957. Jack's grandfather Patrick O'Shea was a farmer from nearby Laharn, while his father, John, apprenticed as a harness-maker. 'He made harnesses for all the horses and donkeys,' says Jack. 'He did everything with his hands and I watched him and learned from him.'

With the introduction of tractors, harness-making went on the slide, so John moved to Cahersiveen and became a builder. However, while working on the new technical school there, he badly damaged his back and, at the age of 31, was suddenly unable to work.

Jack, then 13, and his older sister, Mary, quickly went to work to bring in vital money for their mother, Bridie, and four younger siblings. Jack began making cartons to package mackerel at the local fish factory for £13 a week. In 1973, a plumber who lived nearby invited him to do an apprenticeship. Five years later, Jack arrived in Dublin and began working as a plumber for another Kerryman called Mick O'Donoghue.

Meanwhile, his footballing career was gathering considerable momentum. 'Where I come from, football is the only thing,' he explains. 'Everybody wanted to play for Kerry. As a boy, I would watch Mick O'Connell and Mick O'Dwyer train in the field opposite

my house two or three days a week. I used to be their ballboy every now and then. Mick O'Connell would come in by boat from Valentia and Mick O'Dwyer would come in from Waterville. They'd train for a couple of hours, mostly kicking and catching. I'd be watching and trying to do what they did.'

The Christian Brothers in Cahersiveen also did their bit. Jack credits them with encouraging him and his classmates to follow their footballing dreams, urging them to practise on Wednesday afternoons, in the evenings, at weekends. 'Some of the priests would get very involved in organising games for us,' he recalls. 'And I'm not sure what it was we were eating, but we became a very good team.'

Jack and several of his classmates signed up with the Cahersiveen club, St Mary's. Under the management of Paddy Murphy, Cahersiveen stormed the Kingdom for the next eight years. 'We won a lot of the South Kerry championships,' says Jack. 'We won Under-12, Under-14, Under-16, the minor . . . we were the same team all the way through. Three of us from the club won All-Irelands together, but I was the only one who won as a senior.

'It was all innocent fun. Everything was about exercise and it was all natural. I never got injured or pulled a muscle when I was playing, which is very unusual for the amount of football I played. My physio said it was because I was physically working on the Monday after a match, plumbing, jumping into attics, jumping on sites, automatically stretching . . . it was all physical, rather than sitting in a car to get to work and then sitting at a desk all day.'

But his fitness was not all down to being a plumber. It undoubtedly helped that he gave up alcohol at the age of 18. He also played badminton regularly and was a cross-country-running champion, once coming fourth to John Treacy. 'But I never went to the gym and I'm not going to start at this stage.'

Jack is scoffish about certain aspects of modern life. 'There's everything too handy now,' he believes. 'People don't appreciate things. They demand everything and want everything. But you can't appreciate things unless you go out and earn them yourself. All our kids are just handed everything. If they didn't get what they wanted, I think a lot of them wouldn't be able to cope. It's frightening to say that, but if you ask young people to cook for themselves or change a fuse in a plug or even change a light bulb, a lot of them don't know how. They think the light comes on when you hit the switch and that's it.'

Jack made his minor debut for Mick O'Dwyer's side against Waterford in the 1974 Munster championship. He went on to represent the Under-21s, with whom he played in a record four All-Ireland finals, winning three of them. It was in 1978, the year he moved to Dublin to develop his plumbing career, that he first lined out in the green and gold for the Kerry seniors.

Between 1978 and 1981, he was a key member of the Kerry senior team that won four consecutive All-Irelands. He then managed to be on the team that won the 1984–86 three-in-a-row. It is arguable that no man has ever received louder cheers in Croke Park than he did for the conviction with which he launched into his dazzling high catches. Many of those who queued up at the turnstiles were there because they wanted to see Jack. In 1984 and 1986, he captained the first Ireland teams to play international rules against Australia.

He is the only person in the history of Irish sport to win six All Star awards in a row. In all, he enjoyed a remarkable 16 years before retiring in 1992 after a match in which Clare bridged a 75-year gap to beat Kerry and win their second-ever Munster title.

Jack also played for his local clubs, St Mary's in Kerry and, after he set up business locally as a plumber in 1984, Leixlip in Co. Kildare, with whom he won the Co. Kildare Division One league title. He also managed the Co. Mayo team from 1992 to 1994, which he enjoyed.

These days, he is not particularly sporty, although he plays golf every week and heads out deep-sea fishing whenever he is home in Kerry. He also still enjoys one of the Kingdom's more energetic pastimes, beagling. 'There's a lot of beagle clubs down the Iveragh where I come from,' he says. 'I like to go running up the mountains with the hounds. We hunt hare most of the time, and the odd fox, but we don't catch them. It's good exercise. You'd eat the dinner when you come home.'

Jack presently works as maintenance manager with the Moriarty Group, with particular responsibility for SuperValu and the Bracken Court Hotel in Balbriggan. He is also a regular columnist for the Irish edition of the *Sunday Times* and manager of the South Kerry divisional team. He and his wife Mary have four children. Their sons Aidan and Kieran are both footballers on the rise.

During Kerry's victory over Dublin in the 1985 All-Ireland football final, all eyes were on Jack O'Shea, the plumber from Cahersiveen who scored the Kingdom's opening goal after 11 minutes. Not surprisingly, he was voted Texaco Player of the Year 1985. (© Ray McManus/Sportsfile)

PETER CANAVAN

Gaelic Football

TITLES
All-Ireland: 2
Ulster: 4
National League: 2

AWARDS
All Stars: 6
All Star Footballer of the Year, 1995
Texaco Footballer of the Year, 2003
BBC Northern Ireland Sports Personality of
   the Year, 2003
TG4's Favourite Footballer of the Last 25
   Years, 2009

Prior to his victory at Aintree in 2010, Tony McCoy feared he was going to be recalled as the greatest jockey to never win the Grand National. Much the same label had been pinned to the lapels of Tyrone footballer Peter Canavan when he started his 2003 All-Ireland campaign. Was he destined to go down in the GAA annals as the greatest player to never win an All-Ireland?

He has not yet spent 40 years on the planet, but the Ballygawley PE teacher is the most decorated Gaelic football player Ulster has produced, with a massive scoring record of 218 points, six All Star awards and two extraordinary All-Ireland titles to his credit.

Peter's father, Seán Canavan, was born in 1928 and raised on a 35-acre farm in Greenhill, a few miles north-west of the small village of Ballygawley, Co. Tyrone. One of nine children, Seán ran the farm, as well as a butcher's shop in Ballygawley, for many years. A passionate GAA man, Seán was 32 years old when the Sam Maguire crossed the border for the first time. It was his lifelong hope that it would one day come to Tyrone. He played football for St Ciaran's Ballygawley, as well as some clubs in Monaghan, and later became honorary president of Errigal Ciarán, the club that he co-founded in 1991.

Peter was the tenth of Seán and Sarah's eleven children, raised on the same remote farm and educated locally at St Malachy's Primary School, Glencull. He was generally the most active of the six brothers, always galloping around the yard, hiking the ball into the sky, imagining himself as his heroes and yelling out the Michael O'Hehir commentary as he ran. You can hear one of his amusing commentaries on YouTube, recorded back when he was a squeaky-voiced 12 year old.

And yet, all along, he has been up against it. He's been asthmatic since childhood and,

certainly before medication improved, was frequently short of breath and wheezing. He was nonetheless always fit, not least because, with his brothers, he spent so much of his time working on the farm, feeding the cattle, saving the hay and silage and suchlike.

Asthma wasn't the only hindrance to his underage career. While at St Ciaran's High School in Ballygawley, he made a huge impression on the field, but he was not eligible for selection for the Tyrone minors because his club, Errigal Ciarán Naomh Malachai, was not properly registered with the GAA. Showing the canniness for which he is widely known, Peter bypassed the problem by signing up as a member of the Killyclogher hurling club. He has never played hurling in his life. But at least he was now eligible for selection.

In 1988, he played on the Tyrone team that won the Ulster minor championship, but which was put out of the All-Ireland in the semi-final by Kerry. Peter went on to lead his county to All-Ireland Under-21 wins in 1991 and 1992. By this time, he was studying physical education at St Mary's University College, Belfast.

His selection for the county's senior team was inevitable. His older brother, Pascal, was also on the team and they played together for most of the 1990s. Peter quickly became the team's luminary, winning his first All Star at the age of 23 and marching the county to the 1995 All-Ireland final in Croke Park. And while Tyrone lost to Dublin, 11 of their 12 points came off the boot of Peter Canavan. That year, in fact, he achieved a tally of 1–38, more than any other footballer in the country, and won the newly established Texaco Footballer of the Year award.

In 1996, he captained his county through to a heated semi-final against Meath in which he was one of six Tyrone players wounded. He tore a ligament in his ankle, an injury that was still ailing him a year later.

In 1998, he was corner-forward for Ireland in the first International Rules Series against Australia. The following year, he was vice captain of the team that basically crushed Australia. His 2000 Aussie Rules campaign was marred by a bitter rivalry with Australia's Jason Akermanis that broke into fights during the first two Tests.

In 2002, Peter captained Tyrone to their first National Football League title. They started that year's All-Ireland campaign as one of the tournament favourites, only to be stunned by an early loss to Sligo.

Peter contemplated retiring after the Sligo defeat but held steady and the 2003 campaign began. It was to be an emotional journey. Peter's father Seán died just over a week before Tyrone met Down in the Ulster final. His funeral at Ballymacilroy was an intense experience for his six sons and five daughters. The following Saturday, Peter lined out in honour of his father. For a while, it looked like Down were going to whitewash the Red Hands. Then a penalty kick came Tyrone's way. Peter took it and watched the ball sail into the net. 'That kick was the most important of my career,' says Peter. The match ended in a draw and paved the way for Tyrone to win their first All-Ireland senior football championship.

Peter captained the team for the final but came off with an ankle injury (a split tendon). And then, ten minutes before the final whistle, Tyrone's manager (and Ballygawley native) Micky Harte waved his magic wand and reintroduced Peter to the pitch. The Tyrone crowd roared their approval and Peter's presence inspired the team to a famous victory. He delivered a deeply stirring speech when he finally got the opportunity to lift the Sam Maguire, allowing himself to expunge his many recent experiences of death and injury. 'It took me a long time to get here,' he told the crowd. 'I can't think of a better place or position to be in than right now where I'm standing. It's time to take Sam to Tyrone.'

In the 2004 and 2005 championships, Peter accepted the role of 'impact substitute', meaning that Harte would bring him on at critical moments to inspire the other Tyrone players, fire the crowd and fluster his opponents. And if proof of Peter's ongoing deadliness was needed, in the 2005 semi-final against Armagh he kicked Tyrone through to the All-Ireland final with a single point in the very last kick of the game. He went on to score Tyrone's only goal in the final, as the county won its second championship.

Peter retired from inter-county football after the 2005 victory, after 16 years at senior level in which he played 49 championship matches. 'I've spent enough time on the treatment table,' he explained. He continued to play at club level for Errigal Ciarán until 2007. Over the 17 years during which Canavan played with them, the club won six Tyrone senior titles and two Ulster championships. In 2008, he became manager of the club and led them to victory in the Tyrone All-County League final in 2009.

Throughout his career, Peter retained his job as a PE teacher at the Holy Trinity College in Cookstown. Amongst his students was the remarkable Tyrone forward Eoin Mulligan, and Peter has now gone down in GAA lore as the Jedi Master who taught Mulligan his point-taking tricks. Peter's media work includes regular contributions to GAA magazine

In September 2005, Tyrone recorded their second-ever win in the All-Ireland senior football championship, when, in one of the most astonishing periods in the history of the sport, they rose through the ranks to defeat Kerry in the final. Of all the men who helped Tyrone win the Sam Maguire that day, it is arguable that none had more impact than Peter Canavan, the PE teacher from Cookstown. (© Ray McManus/Sportsfile)

Hogan Stand and the *Daily Mirror*'s Ulster edition, as well as football punditry for TV3.

In 1993, Peter married Finola McGarrity, sister of his Tyrone teammate Ronan McGarrity. They have four children, Áine, Claire, Darragh and Ruairi, all of whom play football for Errigal Ciarán.

ANGELA DOWNEY-BROWNE

Camogie

TITLES
All-Ireland: 12
Leinster: 13
National League: 9

AWARDS
B&I Player of the Year Award, 1977
Texaco Sportstars Award, 1986
GAA Camogie Team of the Century, 2004
Irish Times/Irish Sports Council Lifetime
Achievement Award, 2009

On Sunday, 24 September 1995, Angela Downey-Browne made her way to the dressing-room of the Cork camogie team and stood in the doorway. Silence descended on the room as the Cork players, celebrating their victory over Kilkenny in the All-Ireland final, noticed the petite but immense Kilkenny legend. 'You have waited a long time for this night,' said Angela, when the hush was complete, 'to beat Kilkenny . . . enjoy your night.' It was a typically good-natured and frank sign-off from Ms Downey, considered the greatest player in the history of the game. The following day, the 38-year-old corner-forward announced her retirement from the sport after an astonishing 25 years. She planned to take to the golf fairways, she said, to see if she could get her handicap down from 36.

Between the late 1970s and the early 1990s, Angela and her twin sister, Ann Downey, were the shining stars in a team packed with outstanding players. It was a golden age for camogie in Kilkenny and, notching up a dozen All-Ireland titles, the girls proved themselves practically invincible. Perhaps their most memorable moment was after the 1977 All-Ireland, when Angela, as team captain, grabbed Ann for a massive bear hug on the victory rostrum before raising the O'Duffy Cup high above their heads.

Born in 1957, the Downey sisters were the third and fourth of five children born to Shem and Brigid Downey. Shem ran a butcher's shop in the town of Ballyragget. He had been one of Kilkenny's hurling icons during the 1940s and 1950s, most notably playing forward for the team that won the All-Ireland in 1947. Angela attributes her prowess to her genes and was so young when she first learned how to rise a ball on a stick that she

47

can't even remember those first steps. By the age of nine, both girls were actively and determinedly playing the game. In later years, Angela would hail her father's support as one of the key factors in their success. 'It's Dad who keeps us both going,' she said in 1986. 'I think he gets more enjoyment out of it than we do. He certainly never misses a match.'

By the age of 12, the sisters were playing on the school team for the Presentation College in Castlecomer. In 1970, aged 13, Angela gave a powerful display to help her club team St Paul's in Kilkenny win their first All-Ireland club medal. She remained with St Paul's until the club disbanded in the early 1990s, during which time she racked up an exceptional haul of six All-Ireland club titles and twenty county titles. Angela played her last All-Ireland club match for St Paul's in 1989 and later played alongside Ann for Lisdowney, collecting a further two county titles. She also played for Leinster in the Gael Linn championship, winning ten inter-provincial titles.

By the time she was 15, Angela had impressed the Kilkenny selectors so much that she was fast-tracked onto the county's senior team. As she says herself, she was 'still very much the baby' but she stayed with the team all the way to the 1972 All-Ireland final at Croke Park, where they were beaten by Cork.

Two years later, Angela secured her first All-Ireland title when Kilkenny beat Cork in a Croke Park thriller to capture their first national title. Angela was selected as Player of the Match. Aidan McCarthy of the *Irish Times* described her as showing 'more adeptness with stick and sliotar' than most of the others on the pitch. He singled out her 'inevitably successful dummies' and 'quick acceleration past the defence' as the highlights of the game, attributing the latter to her dalliance with athletics while at St Brigid's College in Callan. Her lightning pace certainly made defences fraught. Writing in the *Irish Times*, Maol Muire Tynan concurred that the 'sheer speed and power' of this 'deceptively diminutive' player made her 'virtually unstoppable'. She always seemed to be within 15 to 20 metres of the goal, dominating from the puck out and firing countless cracking shots into the net and over the bar.

When she left school, Angela went to St Patrick's College, Maynooth, and helped the college team win a league medal. She also continued to play for her club and county. Aside from 'a bit of basketball and squash', she rarely took a break from the game.

Angela played for a Kilkenny team that contested 13 All-Irelands, and won 12 of them. They utterly overwhelmed the opposition and Angela was the linchpin. Ann was also part of that extraordinary journey, proving herself a sparkling high catcher, attack breaker and team weaver. Both girls were on the team that won Kilkenny's first All-Ireland and they also both played for the county's extraordinary seven-in-a row All-Ireland titles between 1985 and 1991.

In 1984, Angela married Ted Browne, 'a rugby man' from Limerick. She herself began work as a geography teacher at Grennan College in Thomastown. Ted manages the school camogie team at Castlecomer Community School. They have two children, Katie and Conor.

In 1985, Angela was one of two player-members appointed to a commission set up by the Congress of Cumann Camógaíochta na nGael (CCnG) to explore all aspects of the sport from finance to refereeing to pitches, for a game that 65,000 women in Ireland were playing at that time. 'In the end, we must remember it's an amateur sport and we're not trying to make any money out of it,' reasoned Angela.

Of particular interest to her was the issue of safety and she urges players, particularly juveniles, to wear helmets with protective grids. 'I always wore a helmet, gumshield and shin guards,' she says, 'but I learned the hard way. Nobody wants to lose too many teeth.'

Angela received the B&I Player of the Year Award in 1977 and in 1986 she became only the third camogie player to win a Texaco Sportstars Award. In 2004, she was named on the Camogie Team of the Century but boycotted the presentation in protest that her sister Ann was not even nominated for the same team. The mistake was not repeated when Angela and Ann Downey both received the Lifetime Achievement Award for their inter-county careers at the *Irish Times*/Irish Sports Council Sportswoman of the Year 2009 awards.

Ann Downey was also nominated for the 2009 CCnG Manager of the Year for her current role as manager of the Kilkenny senior camogie team. She led them to the finals of both the 2009 All-Ireland final and the 2010 National Camogie League.

As for Angela, she continues to teach in Thomastown. And she's got her golf handicap down to 16.

Clad in the amber and black colours of Co. Kilkenny, Angela Downey-Browne prepares to send the sliotar back towards the Cork goal during the 1995 All-Ireland senior camogie final. A last-minute goal by Cork denied Kilkenny victory, but Angela nonetheless racked up an extraordinary haul of 12 All-Ireland titles during her long career. (© Ray McManus/Sportsfile)

MARY SINNOTT-DINAN

Camogie and Badminton

Camogie

TITLES
All-Ireland: 1
Leinster: 4

AWARDS
GAA Camogie Team of the Century, 2004

Badminton

Caps for Ireland: 59
National Ladies' Doubles Titles: 6
National Mixed Doubles Titles: 2
Irish Open Ladies' Doubles Title: 1
Member of Winning Helvetia Cup Team
International Badminton Federation
 Award, 2004

Local leadership is something that modern Ireland often lacks. In times past, every community had a leader. From chieftains and barons, it became priests and police. In each instance, some were good and others bad. One of the finest in Co. Wexford's history was Garda Sergeant Sean O'Connell. In 1960, this native of Cork was transferred to the village of Taghmon, which is pitched upon a ridge in the south-western hills of the county.

Sergeant O'Connell had been involved with Rathnure St Anne's GAA during the glory days of the Rackard brothers. It occurred to him that when the young people of Taghmon were not at school or working on their family farms, they were inclined to thumb-twiddling. There wasn't a lot to do in the area. The sergeant consulted John Sinnott, a farmer from nearby Aughfad. The two men, and several others, joined forces to construct a new handball alley for the village. When not on the beat, the sergeant was also a badminton enthusiast, and so he ensured that the court was marked out with the necessary lines for a badminton game.

'It's the fastest racket sport in the world,' says Mary Sinnott-Dinan authoritatively. For six years in a row, she was Ireland's ladies' doubles champion. Since 2002, she has also trained the Co. Wexford team to four All-Ireland victories.

Mary is the only daughter of the sergeant's friend, the late John Sinnott. Her family have been in Wexford for many long centuries. For the past 300 years, they have farmed at Aughfad and lived in an ancient schoolhouse that was converted into a home in the early eighteenth century. Not all Sinnotts stayed in Aughfad. In 1851, for instance, two Sinnott

brothers left for America. One became Colonel Nick Sinnott, an iconic hotel owner in Oregon, whose son was elected senator of that state.

Mary's grandfather, Nicholas Sinnott, was born a decade after his namesake left for America. At that time, badminton had not yet been invented. However, in 1873, when Nicholas was 11 years old, the Duke of Beaufort held a lawn party at his country pile, Badminton House in Gloucestershire. Guests were invited to play a game called Poona, imported from British India, in which players used a paddle, called a battledore, to hit a shuttlecock over a net. The guests adored this new pastime and christened it 'the Badminton game'.

But badminton was not for Nicholas. He preferred Gaelic football. In 1886, he lined out for Taghmon against Kilmannon for an epic match in which, as one participant later recalled, Taghmon 'beat themselves by tasting well but not wisely of the many good things that were loaded into the wagonettes and cars in the field'.

In 1940, Nicholas's son John married Mai O'Connor, with whom he would later run the family farm, tending the dairy cows, harvesting the grain. Their only daughter, Mary, was born in 1943, midway between two boys, Nicholas and Sean.

Mary's childhood was set against a golden age for the Wexford hurlers. Her uncle Mick O'Hanlon was corner-back on the team that won the All-Ireland in 1955 and 1956. Her neighbour Jim Morrissey was also on the team and in 1956 it was Jim who whacked the sliotar up the field to Tom Ryan, who shipped it over to Nicky Rackard, who banged it into the Cork net and thereby won the day.

And thus sport became Mary's childhood. 'I used to be always out in the fields hurling with my two brothers,' she recalls. 'We didn't have television or computers, so it was all outdoors. There was very little else to do, except play cards. I played camogie, tennis, hockey and badminton. We enjoyed it and we got great fun out of it.'

Mary was 17 years old when Sergeant O'Connell began pacing around the kitchen at Aughfad, talking about handball courts and badminton. 'He was an absolutely fantastic man. We owe him a lot for what he did for the village. He knew everything that was going on. He tried to get all the youngsters into sports. If one of them did something wrong, he'd bring them in and give them a tap on the ear. He didn't charge them and that was the end of it. You'd never hear of any trouble.'

Educated at the Loreto Convent in Wexford, Mary continued to play badminton after she left, frequently practising on the handball court in Taghmon. She quickly ascended the ladder and showed herself to be a player of considerable dynamism and style. On one particularly memorable occasion in 1967, she won Co. Wexford's senior and junior singles, doubles and mixed doubles titles, all in the same evening. She went on to win the Munster senior singles and doubles titles, securing her place on the Munster provincial side. One fellow player by name of Gay Dinan was so impressed that he proposed to her. Mary and Gay had been seeing each other since 1962; they were wed in Taghmon in 1968.

However, badminton had to take something of a back seat as Mary's camogie career was simultaneously flourishing. She was regarded as one of Co. Wexford's most consistent players and, for a long time, was hailed as the best full-back in Ireland. In 1968, she put in a particularly brilliant performance to help the Model County win its first O'Duffy Cup. She also played for Leinster for ten years, winning Gael Linn medals in 1962 and 1965.

One ebullient match commentator for the *Irish Independent* enthused that Mary had stood 'head and shoulders over every other player on the field . . . grabbing the ball out

of the air, forcing her way past opponents to get seventy and eighty yard clearances . . . connecting with the most difficult ground and air shots to clear many dangerous situations and in a race for the sliotar leaving many opponents standing, she proved that the title of Ireland's best camogie player is hers beyond doubt'.

Following their marriage, Mary and Gay moved to Dublin. Mary signed up with the Clanna Gael Fontenoys and continued to play camogie for her county but, following the birth of their daughter Elizabeth in 1969, she set the stick aside and began to concentrate solely on badminton.

She started at the Pembroke Club at a time when standards were high. 'It was very hard to break into it,' she says, 'but I persisted.' And gradually the young lady from Wexford worked her way up to secure a place on the Leinster team. She later moved to Kadca, with whom she won the Irish Open and six national titles. She won her first international cap in 1975, against the Netherlands, and went on to represent Ireland another 58 times. In 1981, she was one of the seven players who made history in Norway when Ireland won Europe's coveted Helvetia Cup.

In 1983, she announced her retirement, having rather epically just won both the ladies' doubles (with Wendy Orr) and the mixed (with John Scott) to seal Ireland's first victory over England since 1903.

From 2002 to 2009, Mary was trainer of the Wexford badminton team. 'I drove down from Dublin every Friday night from October until the All-Ireland was over in May,' she says. 'But we did well. We won four All-Irelands and five Leinster titles.' Also amongst those she has coached is Sonya McGinn, who became Ireland's first Olympian badminton player at the Sydney Games in 2000.

'I like to win and I hate losing,' says Mary. 'I'm competitive at everything I do and while I don't show it, if I lose, I am seething inside. But aside from that, I love playing badminton. It's good to get out in the evening and take your frustrations out on the shuttle! And it keeps you very fit. For 90 minutes, you're constantly moving. The shuttle can't bounce, so you've got to get there first, and the shuttle can be going at speeds of up to 120 miles an hour. If you're not fit, you might as well stay at home.'

Mary Sinnott-Dinan and her partner Billy Cameron in action at the 1980 Ulster Open in Belfast, where the duo were Ireland's mixed doubles badminton top seeds. (Courtesy of Patrick Lynch)

CORA STAUNTON

Ladies' Gaelic Football

TITLES
All-Ireland: 4
National League: 3

AWARDS
All Stars: 7
Vodafone Ladies' Footballer of the Year,
2000
Irish Tatler Sportswoman of the Year, 2003
Ladies' Football Golden Boot Award, 2007,
2009

'I'm not sure we will ever get the same recognition as men,' sighs Cora Staunton. 'I think it's the same in all sports, except athletics. When women play football or camogie or soccer, there's never the same fan base that men's sports have. So we don't have the same money. That's why our players are always fund-raising on the roadsides so they can buy tracksuits and so on. I'm the only player I know of who's actually been given stuff to wear by a sponsor.'

With seven All Stars to her name, Cora is undoubtedly the greatest ladies' footballer of the modern age. The Mayo sharpshooter has played for her county since the age of fourteen, during which time she has brought home four All-Ireland medals, three National League titles and three more for her club, Carnacon. Between junior, senior, club and county championships, the 28 year old has played in 25 All-Ireland finals. She remains one of the most dominant players in the game and looks set to keep at it for many years to come.

Cora descends from an Anglo-Norman family who settled in Ireland in the wake of Strongbow's tumultuous invasion of AD 1169. Like many an invader, the de Stauntons gradually Hibernicised, forming a clan after the Irish fashion. One branch obtained extensive possessions in Carra, Co. Mayo, the barony in which Castlebar town is situated.

Cora's ancestors lived directly south of Castlebar in Srah, near Tourmakeady. They farmed along the northern shores of Lough Mask, with the Partry Mountains running to their west. In the late nineteenth century, her great-grandparents Michael and Margaret Staunton upped sticks and moved north-east across Lough Carra to a farm between the

ruins of Castlecarra, a mighty thirteenth-century Staunton tower house, and Ballintubber Abbey.

Cora's grandfather James Staunton was born in Castlecarra in 1903, the eighth of ten children. James, a boy when his father died, later married Mary Heneghan, daughter of Walter and Bridget Heneghan, a farming couple who moved to Castlecarra after the First World War, having spent some time in the USA.

Fast-forward to 1981 and the Stauntons of Castlecarra were celebrating the birth of a girl, Cora. She grew up on the family farm, where she was one of eight children, four boys and four girls. Her father, Michael, maintained a herd of dairy cattle, so there was always milking to be done. That said, laughs Cora, 'I was the second youngest, so I was maybe a bit more spoilt and I got out of it.'

The family suffered a considerable tragedy in 1998 with the death from cancer of Cora's mother, Mary. Cora, then 16 years old, remembers her with great affection. 'She was quite strict but very house-proud and a very loving and caring mother. She and my

Co. Mayo's Cora Staunton slips past Laois captain Angela Casey during the 2001 All-Ireland ladies' football final at Croke Park. Laois went on to win the championship, but Cora helped Mayo record back-to-back All-Ireland wins in 2002 and 2003. (© Brian Lawless/Sportsfile)

father worked extremely hard to provide for the eight of us.' Mary, who worked as a catering assistant in Mayo General Hospital when her children had left school, had been raised by a family nearby. It was only after Mary's demise that the Stauntons discovered she had been adopted. 'I don't think she wanted to find out who her parents were, so we will leave it be,' says Cora.

'I always had a football in my hand for as long as I remember,' she says. 'That's all I did when I was young, kicking it – at school, in the garden, everywhere.' At the age of seven, she went to Carnacon National School, where she leapt at the chance to compete in sports of every kind. 'Basketball, soccer, rounders, racketball, handball, anything I could play. I was known as a tomboy because I was the only girl who played all the boys' games.'

Cora's older siblings went to secondary school in the town of Balla. 'I broke the mould,' she says. 'I went to Ballinrobe Community School because it had girls' football, and the school in Balla didn't have such things as girls' competitions!' Her new school lay at the southern end of Lough Carra and was already well known as a nursery for Gaelic footballers, men and ladies alike.

For Cora, it was hugely exciting to find herself in a school with other girls who played sport at such a high level. She quickly made her presence felt and at the start of the 1999 season she was one of seven Ballinrobe girls who were selected for the county team. She excelled from the outset, playing a pivotal role on a team that went on to win Mayo's first-ever All-Ireland with a historic victory over reigning champions Waterford.

Cora broke her collarbone in an accidental collision with a teammate while training a week before the final, so she was unable to compete in the game. However, the Mayo management decided to bring her onto the pitch for the first 90 seconds so that she could be accorded the honour of having played in an All-Ireland final. In a 2009 article for the *Mayo News*, goalkeeper Denise Horan remembered this as 'perhaps the single greatest symbol of unity' for the team. 'No one questioned how sacrificing a sub so early on might impact on the final outcome. Things like that were secondary.'

Mayo won the title. And, as it happened, Cora lined out for the county again the following year when they won a second All-Ireland. The women of Co. Laois got the better of them in 2001, but Mayo returned to win back-to-back All-Ireland titles in 2002 and 2003. Cora was on the team every time, just as she was when Mayo were beaten by Cork in the 2007 final. She was also the sport's top scorer in 2007 and 2009.

When not playing for her county, Cora is busy both coaching and playing for her local club, Carnacon. Indeed, with Cora at the helm, Carnacon have won the Ladies' All-Ireland Club Championship twice in the last four years.

'I keep myself in shape and stay fit all year round,' she says. 'There's only a two-week break between the seasons, so I'm in training all the time. You just don't have a social life for nine or ten months of the year, which is hard. Or if you do socialise, you suffer for it when the season begins. There's plenty of time for socialising when you're 30-plus.'

Cora likes to have a ball in her hand all the time, 'like I did when I was young'. She works out in the gym three days a week and goes for a short-distance jog almost every day.

Part of Cora's extraordinary drive stems from her own unflinching self-critiques. After many a game, while the crowds are still cheering her mighty kicks, she will be mulling over what went wrong with those that she missed.

Gifted she may be, but the Mayo star has not been immune from injury. There is hardly a bone or ligament in her body that has not received some class of a knock, strain, rip or sprain. 'I've been playing with Mayo since I was 14, so that takes its toll,' she says. 'I can safely say that by the time I'm 40 I'll definitely have arthritis and all that. You don't think about it when you're younger. You say, "Oh, I'm fine, I'll keep going." But now I'm older, I think, "God, am I going to be crippled?"'

She says she is philosophical about this rather daunting destiny, reasoning that 'you just deal with it . . . I sometimes wonder how long I can keep going, but it doesn't deter me. I might suffer in ten years' time, but I will play on because you don't know how anything will be in ten years.'

In recent years, ladies' football has gone international. The GAA organise a biannual expedition in which two 'dream teams' comprising the sport's top 30 players embark on an All Stars tour to promote the game abroad. These tours have seen Cora perform on pitches from Singapore to Dubai to San Francisco, where, in the spring of 2010, she bagged 2–5 for the 2008 All Stars to help them defeat their 2009 counterparts.

Cora now works with Mayo as a primary health care coordinator, helping the travelling community understand the importance of health and fitness. As well as coaching and playing football, she plays soccer and handball. In soccer, she won a senior cup medal playing for Mayo and has been capped for the Republic of Ireland. In 2009, she paired up with Roscommon's Deirdre Donohue to win the Ladies' 60 x 30 Handball Showdown.

MICHEÁL Ó MUIRCHEARTAIGH

GAA Commentator

AWARDS
Jacob's Award, 1992
PPI Sports Broadcaster of the Year, 2002
Grand Marshal of Dublin's St Patrick's Day Parade, 2007
Honorary President of the Asian GAA
Sports Ambassador, Institute of Technology Sligo, 2010

In 1939, one of the most spine-tingling events in the history of Croke Park took place when nearly 40,000 hurling fans crowded into the stadium to watch Cork and Kilkenny battle it out for the McCarthy Cup. As the second half got under way, an extraordinarily loud thunderclap stunned the audience, to be swiftly followed by an epic lightning storm. The gallant players continued on, with Kilkenny emerging as winners by a point. But for anyone wondering what the thunder might have signified, they had only to look at the next morning's newspapers. That same day, the British Prime Minister Neville Chamberlain declared that the war with Hitler's Germany had begun.

Amongst those huddled over a wireless listening to the match commentary was nine-year-old Micheál Ó Muircheartaigh. He had listened to his first final the previous year and had become instantly hooked on the sport.

Six years later, the fifteen-year-old farmer's son moved from the Christian Brothers School in Dingle to Coláiste Íosagáin, an Irish-language preparatory school in the Múscraí Gaeltacht of south-west Co. Cork.

The Ó Muircheartaighs, or Moriartys, have been based in Kerry for as far back as time recalls and trace their ancestry to Domhnall, King of Munster. In 1598, Owen Ó Muircheartaigh, head of his clan, was hanged on the gibbet at his own front door by Elizabethan soldiers. The Moriarty lands were simultaneously forfeited to the English Crown.

Such stories had a powerful resonance in the childhood home of young Micheál. His grandfather's grandfather had once farmed lands around Anascaul on the Dingle Peninsula but was evicted during the 1830s. By 1852, Daniel Moriarty was farming 53 acres along the craggy coast of Dún Síon, east of Dingle, where Ignatius Moriarty, Micheál's grandfather, was born that same year.

Ignatius was the only member of the Irish-speaking household not to emigrate to America. His brother Tim, for instance, made a small fortune as a gold prospector in Montana. America was also to be the destination for six of Ignatius's eight children. 'All bar my father and the youngest son went across,' says Micheál. 'The vast majority who emigrated in those days never returned and the main reason for that was simply that the length of time they got for their annual holidays would have been exhausted by the two-way travel by boat.'

Micheál's father, Timothy, was born in 1890. 'He stayed in Kerry because he was inheriting the farm at Dún Síon.' The farm, where Micheál was born in the summer of 1930, was good land and made for a fine living.

However, young Micheál's ambition was not to farm but to teach. In 1948, he entered the teacher-training college of St Patrick's in Drumcondra, Dublin, one of the most influential third-level colleges in Ireland for Gaelic games.

He graduated in 1950 and spent the next 30 years working full time as a teacher with the Christian Brothers in both primary and secondary schools. He simultaneously began playing football for the Geraldines in Dublin. 'There was hardly a Dublin-born person on the team at that time,' he says. 'It was nearly all Kerry and Cork people who were living in Dublin.'

Listening to the Croke Park matches on the wireless was, as for many of his generation, one of the highlights of Micheál's childhood. From St Patrick's, he attended his first match at Croker in 1948, standing in the Cusack Stand to watch Cavan's Gaelic footballers beat Mayo on a very windy day. 'It was the strongest wind I ever remember. At half-time, Mayo hadn't scored and Cavan had three goals and two points. They changed ends and, with the wind, Mayo challenged strongly. The end was very dramatic. Mayo were awarded a 14-yard free at an angle to the right. They were one point in arrears as Padraic Carney kicked, but Cavan's Mick Higgins advanced and fielded the ball. Cavan were winners on a 4–5 to 4–4 scoreline.'

The fact that Micheál can still recall such relative minutiae 62 years after the event took place would surprise nobody who knows him. No man has a more encyclopaedic knowledge of the sport than Micheál Ó Muircheartaigh. He appears to know who won every championship, and the accompanying scores, since the GAA was founded 126 years ago. 'Well, I keep an eye on things,' he says bashfully.

He also knows the background of every GAA event from the disastrous 'American Invasion Tour' of 1888 (when 40 per cent of the touring players jumped ship to remain permanently in the USA) to Tex Austin's seven-day International Rodeo at Croke Park in 1924.

All this knowledge would prove supremely useful when he began his career as a commentator in early March 1949. His audition took place during the first hurling match the Kerryman had ever seen. His passion impressed those listening so much that Radio Éireann asked him to provide an all-Irish commentary for the 1949 Railway Cup football final on St Patrick's Day.

Before long, Micheál was doing all the Irish and English match commentaries on the radio, as well as the Irish-language commentary for the televised minor matches. When Micheál's idol, legendary RTÉ commentator Michael O'Hehir, retired in the mid-1980s, Micheál was the natural heir to succeed him as the station's premier radio commentator.

GAA commentators are well known for their wit, and Micheál is arguably the quickest of them all, rattling out the one-liners quick as blinks. For instance, 'Pat Fox has it on his hurl and is motoring well now . . . but here comes Joe Rabbitte hot on his tail . . . I've seen it all now, a Rabbitte chasing a Fox around Croke Park!' Or, 'Teddy McCarthy to John McCarthy, no relation, John McCarthy back to Teddy McCarthy, still no relation.' And while watching former Cork captain Seán Óg Ó hAilpín race up the pitch, he managed to tell listeners, 'His father's from Fermanagh, his mother's from Fiji, neither one of them a hurling stronghold.'

At the age of 80, this agile and immensely likeable man, the recipient of a number of honorary doctorates and fellowships, as well as a Kerryman of the Year award, has seen an immense amount of change. In times gone by, he often sat up late talking with one of the Dublin footballers who was on the pitch when the British troops opened fire on Bloody Sunday. But he was among those who welcomed rugby and soccer into Croke Park and viewed it as a sign of modern Ireland's maturity. 'Many were overcome by the occasion,' he observes.

He is also much impressed by the manner in which the Gaelic spirit has now gone east and he is Honorary President of the Asian Gaelic games. 'I think it's all about looking ahead rather than looking back,' he says. 'It's about how we can keep it all going for the next generation to enjoy.'

GAA commentator Micheál Ó Muircheartaigh pictured during the 1999 All-Ireland club finals at Croke Park, where he was honoured for his 50 years in broadcasting. (© Brendan Moran/Sportsfile)

JACK KYLE

Rugby

CAPS
Ireland: 46
British and Irish Lions: 6

TITLES
Grand Slam: 1948
Triple Crown: 1948, 1949
Five Nations Championship: 1948, 1949, 1951

AWARDS
OBE, 1959
International Rugby Hall of Fame, 1999
Irish Rugby Football Union Greatest Ever Irish Rugby Player, 2002
International Rugby Board Hall of Fame, 2008

In 1966, a compact, dark-haired Ulsterman strolled from his house in the Zambian town of Chingola and mopped his brow. Jack Kyle, Ireland's legendary out-half, had just arrived in the town to take up his position as a consultant surgeon with the Anglo American Corporation. He would remain in Chingola for nearly thirty-five years, during which time the town was transformed into one of Zambia's biggest cities. Central to the local economy was a copper mine with a vast open-cast pit, the second biggest in the world, which was opened in 1943 and run by the AAC.

'There were two hospitals in Chingola when I got there,' recalls Jack. 'They were open to everybody, not just the miners and their families, so life was busy, interesting and extremely challenging. There were very few surgeons, so we just had to do the best we could. We often had to refer to journals and books for procedural information.'

Although Zambia was one of the few former British colonies that avoided a military coup, the copper industry was rocked by a crash in global prices in 1973 and the subsequent nationalisation of the industry. The AAC became Zambia Consolidated Copper Mines. The option was there for Jack to leave, but he decided to stay on.

John Wilson Kyle was born in Belfast in 1926. His father, John, was the only child of a master baker from Draperstown, Co. Derry. Shortly after the First World War, John senior was employed by the Edinburgh-based North British Rubber Company to oversee their operations in Ireland. The company produced everything from tyres to golf balls to rubber boots. He duly met a company employee called Elizabeth Warren,

whom he married in 1924. Two sons and three daughters followed.

Rugby was not a part of Jack's father's life at this stage but his sons were to change that. First, Jack's elder brother, Eric, got an Irish trial and played for Ulster. And second, Jack made his inter-provincial debut for Ulster schools against Leinster in 1943. By then, Jack was at the Belfast Royal Academy, where he came under the influence of the headmaster, Alec Foster, who had captained Ireland and travelled with the Lions to South Africa in 1910. Jack watched his first international at Ravenhill in 1939, when Wales beat Ireland 7–0. 'I never imagined that one day I'd be wearing the green jersey.'

In October 1944, he entered Queen's University, Belfast, to read medicine, and began to play rugby for a junior XV. One day he was seated in chemistry class when he heard that his rival at out-half had just broken his leg. It was a lucky break, if you will, for Jack, who secured the coveted position and established himself on the 1st XV. He remained on the first team for the rest of his time at Queen's. In 1991, he received an honorary doctorate from the university.

His first major game was playing for an Irish XV against the British Army at Ravenhill in December 1945. He was issued with a green jersey before the match, with a warning that if it was not returned immediately after the game, he would be charged for it.

Green was the colour for Irish players, north and south of the border. 'There was never any religious or political controversy amongst the players,' he says. 'That was the wonderful thing about it. When the various unions were splitting up, the Irish Rugby Union said, "We play as one country." Those of us from Ulster were very fortunate that happened. It was also a much greater honour for us to play for the whole country and not just a part of it. I think it says a lot that during all the Troubles, never once did a southern side fail to come north or a northern side fail to go south.'

The green-jerseyed Jack Kyle quickly became one of the linchpins of the Irish team. In 1948, he was on the team that won the historic Grand Slam. He was hailed as the presiding genius when Ireland again scooped the Triple Crown the following year. In 1950, he proved one of the shining lights of the British Lions during their tour of New Zealand and Australia, scoring a try against both. Arguably his most famous try was a solo run against France in 1953, immortalised in a parody of lines from *The Scarlet Pimpernel*:

> They seek him here, they seek him there,
> Those Frenchies seek him everywhere,
> That paragon of pace and guile,
> That damned elusive Jackie Kyle.

At the time of his last appearance for Ireland in March 1958, Jack's total of 46 caps from 11 seasons, yielding 7 tries, was a world record. During those years and later, he concentrated on his surgical career and took the exams to become a specialist surgeon.

From 1962 until 1964, he worked as a surgeon in Sumatra in Sukarno's Indonesia. In 1966, he moved to Zambia, where he remained until 2000. 'People tend to forget what it's like in Africa, but you have to admire the way people manage without any of the social benefits we get here.' In 2007, Jack was honoured with a lifetime achievement award from the *Irish Journal of Medical Science* and the Royal Academy of Medicine in Ireland.

He never lost his passion for rugby and in Zambia he was frequently to be found with an ear to the wireless, listening to match commentaries on the BBC World Service. Talking

about the professionalisation of rugby, he likens it to the winds of change that swept through Africa in the 1960s. 'It was inevitable. It had to happen.'

Naturally, Jack has some reservations about the way the game has gone. 'I started my international career in 1947. I thought about that when I met Brian O'Driscoll because, for him, it must have been like if I'd met someone who'd played in 1884. And I suppose old guys will always thunder on about how things should never have changed.'

So much has changed. For one thing, players have much more of a public profile. In Jack's day, nobody on the team was permitted to give interviews, write for a paper or publish a book. 'We were amateurs,' he says simply.

As for the game itself, 'It's a lot less open than it was. Kicking is now such a large part of it. In the amateur days you place-kicked with the point of the toe, with specially constructed toecaps if desired. If you got the ball over from the ten-yard line, that was considered a terrific kick.'

Aside from the sheer physicality and speed of the modern game, he is astounded by how much the ball itself has changed. When he played, the weight of the leather ball was somewhat controlled by the gods, since it absorbed rain and mud as the game went on. 'The first time I felt the ball the guys play with today, I couldn't believe how light it was.'

Today, Jack lives in the Co. Down village of Bryansford and strolls now and again amid the beautiful 630-acre Tollymore Forest Park, with its sumptuous views from the mountains of Mourne down to the sea. In 2001, he gave his name to the Jack Kyle Bursary Fund in support of the Queen's University RFC Rugby Academy. He has a son, a daughter and three grandchildren.

Jack Kyle (third from left) sits with other members of the Irish rugby team on the eve of their 3–0 victory over England in the 1951 Five Nations Championship. Ireland went on to win the series.
(© Fox Photos/Hulton Archive/Getty Images)

WILLIE JOHN McBRIDE

Rugby

CAPS
Ireland: 63
Lions: 17

TITLES
Five Nations Championship: 1974

AWARDS
MBE, 1971
Texaco Sportstars Hall of Fame, 1995
International Rugby Hall of Fame, 1997
Heineken Rugby Personality of the Century, 2004
RTÉ/Irish Sports Council Hall of Fame, 2005

Some years ago, thumbing through a pile of archives in Ballymena's museum, Willie John McBride came across a photo, dated 1920, of an impeccably dressed man standing beside an Irish swing-plough and two horses. He recognised the landscape, and particularly the flax dams in the back of the shot, as the family farm at Moneyglass, near Toomebridge, close to the north-west shores of Lough Neagh. 'When I was 15 years old, I was down at that same dam at five o'clock every morning, throwing the flax up onto the banks to dry.' The man in the photo was Robert McBride, his grandfather. Willie John had never seen him before.

William James McBride was born at Moneyglass in 1940. His father had lately succeeded to the farm but when Willie John was four years old, he 'literally just dropped dead . . . He'd fallen off a horse and hurt his leg, so they think it might have been a clot that got him. I always remember him with a stick.'

Fortunately, his mother was a resilient soul. She took on the farm and assigned jobs to her four small children. 'When school was done, we came home and went to work,' recalls Willie John. 'Feeding the pigs, collecting eggs, cutting turf. We'd milk the cows before we went to school. It was all horses. No machinery. Aye, different times but it did us no harm at all. That's how you build strong men, not in a gymnasium.'

'I was never in a gym in my life,' growls the five-time Lions champion and former Irish captain. 'But I guarantee that I was stronger than any of the guys playing rugby today. We didn't have substitutes in my day. If you were hurt, you didn't let on because if you came

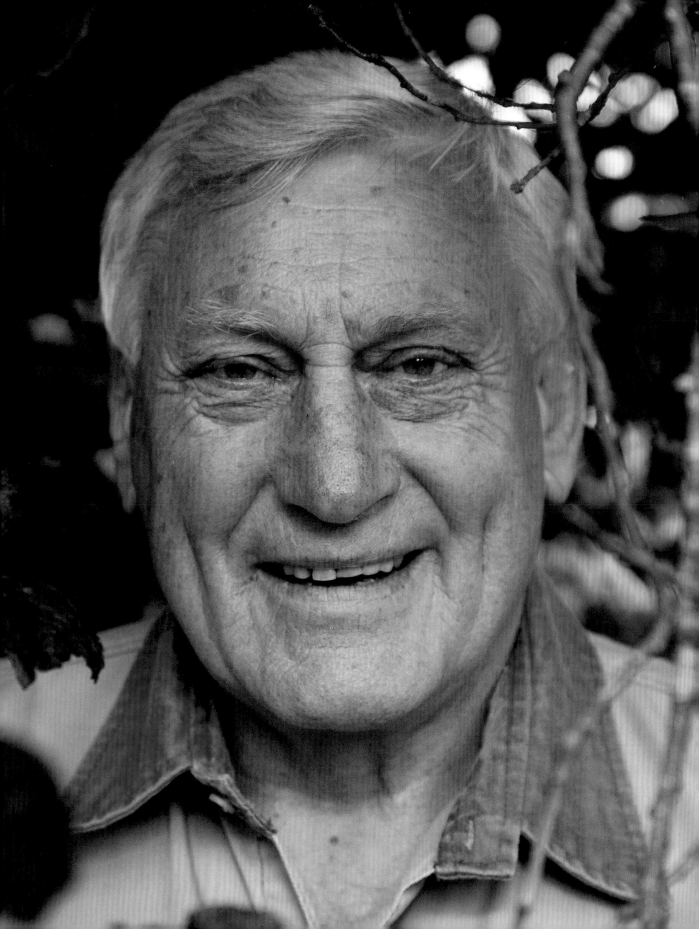

off, you only left 14 men on. Oh, yes, we could take punishment. There is no question in my mind that we were tougher than they are now.'

The press loved Willie John – no surname required. The pipe-smoking gentle giant from the land of Finn MacCool. The bitter-swilling lock forward who made buildings shake and hotel managers tremble with the rumble of his laugh. He was one of the dominant rugby players in the world throughout the 1960s and 1970s. He played for Ireland 63 times, 12 as captain, including historic wins against both the Springboks and New Zealand. And yet he scored only one try for the country, and that was in his last season.

He was perhaps as well known for his contribution to the British and Irish Lions tours, taking part in a remarkable five tours, with seventeen Lions Tests, becoming the most capped player in the series. He captained the last of those tours, during which the Lions tore South Africa apart, winning 21 of their 22 games. It was a controversial tour from the start, not least because the Irish skipper decided the best way to tackle the aggressive antics of the South African players would be to 'get our retaliation in first'. That resulted in the now legendary '99' call; whenever Willie John yelled out that magic number, every Lion on the pitch was to wallop his nearest rival as frequently as possible for the next 30 seconds. It wasn't pretty but it worked, and the Lions returned home bronzed and triumphant to be greeted by Welsh choirs, champagne breakfasts and a gift of a lion cub from Lord Bath.

To the anti-apartheid activists who reckoned the Lions should never have gone to South Africa in the first place, Willie John replied, 'I'm a rugby player not a politician.' He pointed out that rugby had been one of the greatest uniting factors in troubled Ireland. 'They were great days,' he says, 'great guys.'

Willie John is mowing the lawn when we arrive and itching to get stuck into some hedge cutting. 'I love working with the soil,' he says. 'It's in my bones.' At the back of his home in Ballyclare lies a lush and well-kept garden: springy lawns, admirable borders, feisty copper beeches and sturdy saplings. Free-range chickens scamper anxiously beneath a knoll upon which a pair of donkeys drolly munch upon the grasses. A granddaughter bounces skywards on a nearby trampoline. Willie John walks through his garden, proudly pointing out his bumper crop of spinach and sweetcorn, counselling us as to the best way to defeat the carrot fly.

Willie John was the only one of the McBrides to pursue sport. His two brothers still farm in Antrim, while his sister spent more than 40 years in the dermatology department of the Royal Hospital in Belfast.

While at Ballymena Academy, he became a passionate pole-vaulter and, determined to beat an arch-rival, he won the Ulster schools pole-vaulting championship with a leap of 10 ft 9 in. Sean Kyle, who also coached him as a shot-putter and discus-thrower, later stated that Willie John 'could have reached Great Britain standard in both those events but he was wooed away to rugby football'.

At the age of 17, Willie John began to play the sport that made him a household name throughout the rugby-playing world. He started out as lock forward for his school 1st XV and then signed up with Ballymena RFC.

In 1962, he was selected to play his first Test for Ireland against England at Twickenham. 'I got the loan of a jersey and a pair of green socks from the Irish Rugby Union. I was to use the same one for every game I played. If it was ripped or torn, it was over to me to patch it up. And if, at the end of the season, I'd played the four games, they'd give it to me.'

The Ulster forward proved to be as slippery as a Toomebridge eel, as explosive as the diatomite they mined in the hills around his family farm. That summer, the twenty-two year old headed off on the first of his five Lions tours. Destination: South Africa.

By the time he returned from the tour, the young man's eyes had been opened. 'One of the great things about sport is that it gets you around. Africa blew me away. There is a magic about it that you just won't find anywhere else. It gave me a vision of other things that were interesting and important. I always thought I'd be a farmer. But I found farming to be a very closed world. You weren't interested in what happened ten miles up the road. Now, I'm happy to listen to people talk about cattle and sheep, but I don't think I could have handled that.' And so, instead of farming, the big man from Toomebridge focused on his rugby career and joined the Northern Bank, with whom he stayed for 37 years.

As well as his five Lions tours, Willie John played for Ireland in fourteen successive Five Nations championships. In 1974, Ireland won the competition for the first time in 23 years, with Willie John at the helm. A few weeks later, he had just exited Belfast's Northern Bank and rounded a corner when a 500-lb bomb blew the bank apart. Had he stopped to tie a shoelace, the Lions would have been without a captain for their tour to South Africa that summer.

He played his last game for Ireland in 1975 and moved into management, making his way up through the ranks from Ballymena to Ulster to Ireland to manage the Lions themselves.

At the age of 70, he remains an exceptionally busy man, working with numerous charities – he is president of the Wooden Spoon Society in Northern Ireland – and sports award committees, presenting prizes and giving motivational speeches.

'I still believe Ireland is the best little corner of the world,' he says. 'We have a quality of life that I can't see anywhere else. There are changes, of course. The days when we'd go into pubs and talk to the characters behind the bar and have a bit of crack, that's all gone. But I guess it's the same as rugby. It all changes.'

Willie John McBride wins possession for Ireland in a lineout against France during the opening match of the 1965 Five Nations. More than 55,000 packed the stands of Lansdowne Road to watch the match, which ended in a 3–3 draw. Ireland went on to beat England and Scotland, only for Wales to crush their Triple Crown ambitions in the final showdown. (© Connolly Collection/Sportsfile)

PACKIE BONNER

Soccer

CELTIC
Scottish League Championship: 1979, 1981, 1982, 1986, 1988
Scottish Cup: 1980, 1985, 1988, 1989, 1995
Scottish League Cup: 1983

AWARDS
Texaco Special Achievement Award, 1988
Texaco Sportstars Award, 1990
Freedom of Donegal, 2007
Grand Marshal of Dublin's St Patrick's Day Parade, 2010

IRELAND
Caps: 80
European Championships, West Germany, 1988
World Cup, Italia '90, USA '94

When Celtic's goalkeeper made his way onto the pitch, the Italians began to clap. Any player who lines out for a World Cup deserves a degree of applause. But Packie Bonner was the Irishman whose sensational performance between the posts had brought his homeland all the way to the quarter-finals of Italia '90. Sensing that the ovation was for him, Packie bashfully broke into a trot. And then, just as he reached the 18-yard line, he tripped up and fell flat on his face.

'So that was a bit embarrassing,' he laughs, nearly 20 years later, seated in the office of the Football Association of Ireland (FAI), where he now works as technical director.

Italia '90 was undoubtedly the defining moment of Irish soccer, as the 'foreign sport' suddenly brought the country to a standstill. It was also something of a breakthrough in Anglo-Irish relations, with players like Andy Townsend and Mick McCarthy proudly wearing their green jerseys whilst speaking in the broad dialects of Bexley and Barnsley.

But of all the players to capture Irish hearts during that campaign, Packie Bonner was the man. 'They reckon we descended from the French,' he says of the Bonner family. His grandfather, Denis Bonner, was a fisherman and small farmer who lived at Cloughglass, a mile outside the fishing village of Burtonport on the north-west coast of Co. Donegal. His father, Andrew Bonner, also headed out on the trawlers as a young man. 'But the sea didn't agree with him,' says Packie. 'It was a rough old life on the trawlers and he used to get violently sick.'

As such, Andrew did what people from Donegal have been doing since at least the time

of St Columba. He packed his bags and headed for Scotland. 'A lot of people from around where I lived went to work in Scotland,' says Packie. Most fetched up as 'tattie-hokers', crawling through the fields of Girvan, Kirkintilloch and Aberlady, picking potatoes. Others went to the fish factories of Campbeltown. Andrew Bonner sidestepped both fish and spuds, and instead found a variety of jobs, including being a tram conductor in Glasgow. 'He was a very astute man,' says Packie. 'He didn't go to college or university or anything but he was a very quick learner and fantastic with his hands. If there was a problem, he would think it out, and think and think, and eventually he would come up with a solution.'

Andrew later made his way to Edinburgh, where he met and married Packie's mother, Grace Sharkey, who, along with her three sisters, was working in a hotel in the Scottish capital at the time. Their father, Paddy Sharkey, was a fisherman from Mullaghduff, about ten miles from Andrew's family home in Donegal.

The newly-weds made their way to Glasgow, where they spent six months in a house on Copland Road. Their son, the former Celtic goalkeeper, ruefully notes that the house stands along the east side of Rangers' Ibrox Stadium.

During the early 1950s, the Bonners were racked by a series of unexpected and premature deaths, including those of Packie's grandfather and his uncle Packie (for whom he was named) at the age of 21. They returned to Donegal and opened a bed and breakfast for tourists and tradesmen working at Burtonport.

It must have been a tight squeeze because there were already ten Bonners in the house, between Andrew and Grace, Andrew's widowed mother, Margaret, and their seven children, five girls, two boys.

'Burtonport was a fantastic place to be a child,' recalls Packie, who was born in Donegal, along with his twin brother, in May 1960. 'We were right beside the sea, we had boats and we were always out fishing. My cousins fished on the trawlers and used to bring us boxes of turbot and John Dory. It was the best of fish. My dad had lobster pots and fishnets and during the summers the whole family would go out to the rocks and pull dulse seaweed.'

When not at sea, the young Bonners were tending to the animals, cutting turf in the bogs, gathering hay and potatoes. 'It was a very rural Irish childhood,' he says. 'I don't remember rainy days! I just remember lying down in the grass with a blue sky, listening to the birds.'

While there was no telephone in Packie's childhood home, there was a television. And by dint of their proximity to Northern Ireland, the Bonners enjoyed what he calls 'the luxury of BBC and ITV', as well as RTÉ. One of Packie's earliest television memories is watching the 1970 FA Cup final with his father.

'Soccer was very strong in our area,' he says, 'because Ballyshannon was a garrison town so the soldiers would have played the game. Arranmore Island, which we could see from our house, was big on soccer and a number of the islanders actually went to Scotland and played for Hibs.'

Packie and Denis played both soccer and Gaelic football. 'Because we were twins, we always had someone to play with. I'd go into goal and then Denis would go in and, well, I guess I was better than him in goal. And then our next-door neighbour would come around and kick as well. Sometimes Dad took us to see the games at Finn Park.'

In 1970, a good herring season enabled Andrew to purchase football boots for the ten-year-old brothers. The Bonners were soon playing for the local junior club, the Keadue

Rovers, known as 'The Gulls'. When they were 16, the brothers helped the Gulls win Donegal's Under-18 league title and then played Monaghan for the Ulster title. 'Maybe it's because we played Gaelic as well, or because there was a culture of soccer from the area, but we produced a lot of decent footballers.'

But for Packie, his future lay across the water. 'I went to Leicester City for a trial when I was sixteen,' he says, 'and I was over and back to them about six times before they decided not to pick me.'

But the following year, aged 17, he was at school in Dungloe when a soccer scout from Derry pinned him for a trial with Jock Stein's Celtic. 'I was 18 when I arrived, so I had time to finish at school, which was very good for me.'

Packie made his debut at Parkhead on St Patrick's Day 1979. Over the next 12 years, he wore the number 1 jersey for Celtic for a remarkable 642 matches, before they parted ways in 1996. During this time, Celtic won five Scottish League Championships, five Scottish Cups and a Scottish League Cup.

Packie made his international debut for Ireland on his 21st birthday in 1981 against Poland. It wasn't his best game. He conceded the first goal in 90 seconds, followed 36 minutes later by a David O'Leary own goal. But the Donegal man bounced back and went on to win 80 caps for Ireland over the next 13 years. His most vital save in all that time

When Brazil beat Italy to win the 1994 World Cup in the USA, it was widely noted that the Republic of Ireland had also defeated Italy with a terrific 1–0 victory in their opening match of the contest. Central to Ireland's towering performance was Packie Bonner, the goalkeeper from the coast of Donegal. (© Dave Maher/Sportsfile)

was against Daniel Timofte's penalty in the 1990 World Cup shoot-out against Romania. Along with David O'Leary's successful strike, that earned Ireland a place in the quarter-finals. The jubilant scenes that erupted across Ireland in the aftermath of this moment were memorably recreated in the film of Roddy Doyle's book *The Van*.

Being a goalkeeper, Packie had to master the art of staying limber and warm when the ball was up the far end of the pitch. That was vital on the snow-swept pitches of Scotland during his Celtic days. But the hardest game he ever played was Ireland against Mexico in the 1994 World Cup. 'The match was played at midday and it was 130 degrees in the stadium in Orlando,' says Packie. 'And we weren't allowed water!'

A man of seemingly unrufflable composure, Packie says he never had a problem sleeping the night before a match. 'I could sleep for ten hours, to be honest. Then I'd get up, have breakfast, go for a walk and go back to bed in the afternoon before the game. I'd be much more uptight about some of the things I do now than I was playing football.'

'I don't miss the pressure of having to win,' he says. 'I do miss having that fitness level because the nature of my job now is lots of meetings and travel so it's difficult to have a routine. My wife and kids live in Glasgow and I'm based in Dublin for five days a week, so that's not easy. But it does give me a kick that I could come back to my own country and make an impact on creating a great team. A football game was high pressure but it's over in 90 minutes. What I'm doing now is a longer sell – it gives you time to really plan things.'

STEPHEN MARTIN

Hockey

MEDALS
Olympics, 1984, bronze
Olympics, 1988, gold
Champions Trophy, 1984, bronze
Champions Trophy, 1985, silver

CAPS
Ireland: 135
Great Britain: 94

AWARDS
MBE, 1993

'The doctors told me I would never play sport again.' Dr Stephen Martin still grimaces as he recalls that moment when, aged 13, he lay flat on a hospital bed in Bangor, trying to work out what 'complications of the appendix' really meant.

The idea that his sporting career might already be over was something he could not dwell upon. Flashbacks to kicking soccer balls with the Boys' Brigade, gym classes at primary school, heaving mauls on the rugby pitch of Bangor Grammar, strutting out to the greens of the Donaghadee Golf Club with his uncle, scratch golfer Peter Martin.

A thirst for adventure was in his blood. His mother came from Enniskillen, his father from Portadown, and both moved to the coastal town of Donaghadee in the early 1950s. By the time Stephen was born in the spring of 1959, they were living in Bangor on the southern shores of Belfast Lough. Jim Martin, Stephen's father, worked in the motor-racing business. A veteran of the Phoenix Park circuit in Dublin, he worked closely with J.R. Pringle, a garage owner from Bangor who held a number of hill records in Ireland. Jim used to prepare J.R.'s cars ahead of the various championships, including the Formula One Cooper in which Stirling Moss had won the Argentine Grand Prix in 1958.

'I'd go along to all the races with my dad as a three, four and five year old,' says Stephen. 'I loved the smell and the noise and the atmosphere.' In 1962, John Cooper offered Jim a job at the firm's new Formula One base in Surrey. Unwilling to move his young family across the water, he turned the offer down and opened up a garage of his own in Bangor.

Stephen was in his second year at Bangor Grammar School when he received a late diagnosis of appendicitis. After a month in hospital, his recovery was gradual but determined. Initially, he headed out on cross-country runs to exercise his leg muscles. Then he began to stroll onto the fairways with his golfing irons.

'I always thought I was destined to play golf, or maybe soccer, but then I discovered hockey.' His older brother introduced him to the sport. 'He was three years above me and he showed me how to use a stick. I thought, OK, the rules are pretty similar to soccer, I can do this.'

By his fourth year at Bangor, contrary to medical expectations, Stephen had muscled his way onto the school's 1st XI hockey team. That was no mean feat given that there were 800 boys at the school, but he says it was 'a rough year because I was too young'.

He played on the 1st XI again the next year, and the next. He also continued his golfing career and was on the team that won both the Ulster and Irish schools golf championships in 1976 and 1977.

At the age of 17, Stephen lined out for the Ulster hockey team in the Irish schools championship. Two years later, he scored his first cap for Ireland, with whom he went on to play 135 games. That included three European Cups and the 1990 World Cup in Lahore, at which Ireland were ranked 12th in the world.

On account of a loophole in the rules for citizens of Ulster, Stephen was also entitled to represent Great Britain. 'I had the best of both worlds,' he laughs. He won his first cap for GB, as he calls it, in 1983 and went on to win a total of 94.

In the summer of 1984, he went to Los Angeles to play in the Olympics for Great Britain. The team hit a winning streak and came home with Olympic bronze. He also represented Britain at ten Champions Trophy tournaments, winning bronze in 1984 in Karachi and silver in 1985 in Perth, Australia. In 1985, he graduated from the University of Ulster, Jordanstown, with an honours degree in sports studies.

In 1988, he went to the Olympic playing fields of Seoul and helped Great Britain win a historic gold medal, defeating Germany 3–1 in the final. 'From a performance perspective, winning a bronze and a gold at two different Olympics have to be the key moments of my life.'

In 1992, Stephen captained the GB hockey team at the Summer Olympics in Barcelona. They finished sixth. Upon his return, he went into sports administration, securing an early appointment as director of coaching for Ulster Hockey and later in the Performance Department at Sports Council NI.

From 1998 to 2006, he was deputy chief executive at the British Olympic Association, playing a vital role in the success of London's bid for the 2012 Olympics. He was deputy chef de mission for Team GB at the 2000 Sydney, 2002 Salt Lake and 2004 Athens Olympics. The latter was Britain's most successful Olympics in 80 years.

In January 2006, he was promoted to become the first chief executive of the Olympic Council of Ireland. He worked closely with the Irish team for Beijing 2008 and is now involved in planning and preparation for London 2012.

The Olympic Council are based in the Dublin suburb of Howth, where the smell of seaweed and the squawks of gulls roll along the rocks to Stephen's office. North along the coast is Malahide, where he lives with his wife Dorothy (née Armstrong). A part-time teacher at Priory College in Hollywood, Co. Down, Dorothy was pretty handy with a hockey stick herself in times past. She played senior league hockey for Knock and Grosvenor Ladies. They have two children, Patrick and Hannah. Patrick has represented

Ulster at Under-16, Under-18 and Under-21 levels. He is a regular on Lisnagarvey Hockey Club's 1st XI, who finished as runners-up to Pembroke Wanderers in the 2010 Irish Hockey League final. Hannah is currently in the Irish Under-16 squad preparing for the European Youth Championships. 'They both enjoy the team aspect and camaraderie of hockey,' says Stephen.

Stephen's exercise regime in the present age is dictated by the obligations of office life. He aims to fit in an hour's cycling and three thirty-minute runs a week. 'With old injuries, I know how to manage the body better,' he says.

One of Stephen's goals is to make sport more alluring to young people. 'You can waste a lot of money trying to get people involved in sport. It's better to spend the resources on those who want to be involved. Once you've captured people's interest, that's the time to spend time developing it. There's nothing better than a role model. Irish rugby is doing well, so young people are playing rugby. If your county Gaelic team is doing well, more people will play that. When Padraig Harrington wins a major, it helps to fuel interest in golf. People want to be the next sports star. Sports need to have programmes in place to capture that interest.'

He also has a word of advice for those whose sporting career comes to an end when they reach their mid-30s. 'In some sports, money is a factor. But for a lot of sports, you're never going to make your millions and it's more about fulfilling your potential, your sense of achievement. You have to be prepared for the transition when you leave the sport. Athletes should challenge themselves to take on a post-graduate qualification or some part-time work in their area of interest.'

ALAN LEWIS

Cricket

CAPS
121

AWARDS
NatWest Trophy, 1991: Man of the Match
Benson & Hedges Cup, 1995: Man of the Match

BATTING STATISTICS
Record One-Day Score: 127 not out
Runs for Ireland: 3,579 (av. 28.63)
Wickets for Ireland: 51

'It was still seen as a garrison game in my time,' says Alan Lewis. 'A game played by Protestants from little old England. And I suppose it was like a movement. I played against a lot of the sons of the people my father had played against a generation before. But the game has developed hugely in Ireland in the past ten years. It's opened right up and that is fantastic for the sport.'

By 'garrison game', the former Ireland captain means that cricket was one of those 'imported games' favoured by officers of the British Army based in Ireland during the days of the Empire. As such, the founding fathers of the Gaelic Athletic Association condemned cricket as being 'calculated to injuriously affect our national pastimes' and expressly prohibited its members from playing the sport.

By the time the GAA ban was lifted in 1971, seven-year-old Alan was already a regular sight on the YMCA playing fields of Sandymount. 'I was in a pair of pads out in the back garden from when I was three years old. The pads were up to my shoulders, but I could hit the ball OK.'

His love for the sport is genetic. Ian Lewis, his late father, the son of a Dublin haberdasher, played for Ireland 20 times and served as president of the Irish Cricket Union. He grew up in Sandymount and, just as Alan would do, went to St Andrew's College in Booterstown and became an insurance broker. He made his debut for Ireland against the MCC at Lord's in 1955 and won the last of his 20 caps against Canada in 1973.

In the early 1960s, Ian was posted to Cork City, where he met and married Ida Sweetnam, the daughter of a farming couple from Glanmire, West Cork. By 1968, with young Alan and his sister Nicola in tow, the Lewis family made their way, via Athlone, back to Dublin.

'Life in our house was dominated by cricket on Saturdays,' recalls Alan. The family always went to watch Ian play. 'As a ten year old, I'd score and keep the book and

my mother would do the teas. There's very few wives around who would do the tea nowadays!'

As a boy, he ventured with his father to watch the games played at Mount Juliet in the former cricketing stronghold of Co. Kilkenny. He learned to play at school, heading out to the nets at King's Hospital and Belvedere to practise his defences with plastic and, later, real cricket balls. After school, he started playing for the YMCA in Sandymount and began proving himself worthy of a place on the national team.

In June 1984, Alan made an inauspicious debut for Ireland against the West Indies when he went out for a duck. Over the next 13 years, he played a remarkable 121 games for Ireland, 35 of them as captain. He is one of only ten players to have played more than one hundred times for Ireland. He also held what was then the Irish record for a one-day score of 127 not out against Gibraltar.

While he enjoyed his cricketing career immensely, expectations were always limited. 'We'd play one NatWest Cup match against an English county team and really our modus operandi was to try and do as well as we could . . . realistic chances of winning were slim.' Similar odds greeted them when they played internationals against Australia, the West Indies and Zimbabwe. 'Those teams were playing first-class cricket all the time, so their chances of improving were much greater than ours.'

By the time Ireland gained associate membership of the International Cricket Council in 1993, Alan was a regular member of the team. In 1994, he captained Ireland in both the ICC Trophy in Kenya and the Triple Crown Tournament. In 1997, he fulfilled a lifelong ambition to beat professional opposition when he helped Ireland to a famous victory over Middlesex in the Benson & Hedges Cup.

The last major competition in which he played was the Carlsberg ICC Trophy in Malaysia in 1997, a qualification tournament for the 1999 World Cup. Ireland's fourth place was not good enough. Alan, then 32 years old, took this as his cue to retire, which, in hindsight, he feels might have been slightly premature. 'Even though I was still at my peak, I felt I'd achieved all I could at that point.'

He continues to play cricket as a hobby and marvels at the evolution of the sport in Ireland. 'I'm absolutely delighted with where the game has gone. I was there when we beat Bangladesh in the 20/20. And I watched them beat Pakistan in the World Cup. The game has opened up. We've Australians like Trent Johnston and South Africans like Andre Botha playing for Ireland. And more and more of the Irish team are playing professional county cricket in England. That's all good for us because they are going to be on a level where they can compete on the international stage. Sri Lanka got Test match status in 1975 and won the World Cup in 2002. That just shows you what can happen over a short period of time.'

For a brief stint, Alan toyed with the idea of being a rugby player, but that dream ended when he ruptured a knee ligament. Instead, he found himself rising through the ranks as a rugby union referee. He presently referees between 25 and 30 first-class games a year, primarily in the Six Nations, the Heineken Cup and the Magners League. 'The only final I haven't done yet is a World Cup final,' he says.

'I didn't think, oh my God, I want to be a referee,' he insists. 'I hummed and hawed about it, but when I did it, I really enjoyed it. I love the interaction with the players. And it is a good way to stay fit.'

'Refereeing can be a lonely business,' he adds. 'One minute you have sixty thousand people roaring their heads off all around you, the next you're driving home on your lonesome.' He concedes that it is a slightly masochistic profession but enthuses that it is the search for balance that provides the challenge. 'That's the drug, that's what keeps you going. It's about establishing a foothold of control. If players are transgressing, I have to try and persuade them to think a bit differently.'

PEADAR McGEE

Handball

TITLES
All-Ireland Singles: 10
All-Ireland Doubles: 6

Peadar McGee is the first to admit to the terrible irony of how he banjaxed his hand. After he retired from the sport he had dominated for more than twenty years, Ireland's ten-time handball champion set himself up as a firearms dealer just outside his native village of Newport, Co. Mayo. One day, he was cleaning a shotgun. As his right hand passed over the muzzle, the gun most unexpectedly went off. And when Peadar looked at his hand again, a chunk of it was missing.

He got it fixed up and it works usefully enough these days. And if you're out the Mayo way and looking for a shotgun, or maybe some tackle or a fishing rod, then Peadar is your only man. 'Best Prices in Ireland', his business card vows.

Peadar's grandfather, Peter Paul McGee, was an Ulster Catholic from Aughnacloy, Co. Tyrone, who, aged 20, broke with prevailing trends and migrated to Co. Mayo. He found work as a groomsman with the O'Donnell family of Newport House and, in 1910, married Bridget, the local schoolteacher. 'My grandfather was a sort of buckshee vet,' says Peadar. 'I knew him well when I was a young lad. People would come to him when their animals were sick.'

During the 1930s, Peadar's grandparents moved to a farmhouse right beside where he lives today, from where Bridget carried on teaching. 'We'd have been classed as pretty well off in those times,' Peadar says.

His father, Charlie McGee, was Newport's postman for many years. In 1940, Charlie married Kathleen O'Malley from the island of Inishcuttle in Clew Bay. They had seven children. Peadar, their second child and eldest son, was born in 1943.

'Newport was still a very busy port when I was a boy,' he says. 'There were farmers everywhere, and 14 pubs, but there was no dole, so everyone was doing some sort of work or other. It got very busy when the ships arrived with the ESB poles.'

The ESB (Electricity Supply Board) poles began arriving in the 1950s as part of the Rural Electrification Scheme. Inspired by the new dawn of power supply, Peadar became an electrical engineer at the age of 19. 'I was in charge of one of the gangs who were laying everything out and surveying.'

But electricity was not destined to be Peadar's greatest calling in life. In 1948, Charlie McGee brought his five-year-old son down to Newport's riverfront to admire the new handball court that he and some friends had just created from concrete.

'Handball was a big game in Ireland in those times,' says Peadar. 'You hadn't got your televisions or your soccer matches to watch in pubs. And you didn't have a car to go anywhere. So we were all looking for things to do and ways to exercise. Youngsters in them times were much fitter than they are now.'

Handball was his sport of choice, and in 1962 he scored his first national title when he won the junior doubles aged 19. Four years later, he won his first senior All-Ireland singles title. 'Nobody from the province of Connacht or the county of Mayo had done that before,' he says, clearly still delighted. He would go on to win the singles a total of ten times, including a straight run of six years from 1972–77. His personal tally means that Co. Mayo remains fourth in the list of Ireland's top-ten handball counties. Put another way, Co. Mayo have won 17 All-Ireland handball medals, singles and doubles combined, and Peadar McGee holds 16 of them.

'It's something you're born with,' he believes. 'Like the way some people can play whatever they want on an accordion or fiddle. I never trained in my life. I listen to them all now, the young fellows, training, training, training, and then pulling their muscles and straining tendons. I never missed a match in my life through ill health or injury. If I did get injured, I'd ignore it. But I worked hard when I was growing up. During the summers, when I was off school, I was on the salmon boats for Newport House, hauling nets. That's hard work. You'd dig your heels into the ground and pull and you'd gain an inch at a time. I also worked as a relief postman in the summer, cycling around the hills and all. So you build up your muscles that way. I was tough. There's no doubt about it. And I played for stubbornness. I didn't want to give in to anyone. I played hard because I didn't want to lose. It's an in-built thing. It gave me mental pleasure to beat people.'

Peadar had an unusual psychological advantage over his opponents. 'Throughout my career, whenever I went into the fifth game, the tie-breaker, I never lost it. After a while, my opponent would have known this too, so that must have psyched him out every time.'

He says the game has become steadily easier on the players over time and that modern courts are both smaller and better. 'We only ever played outdoors, so the weather played a big part in it. We were running about on hard, cracked concrete floors in canvas slippers, ramming into the walls. And still I haven't a pain in my legs!' He also says that the modern match lasts a good deal less time than it did in his day. 'When I began, there was a rubber [or set] of seven games, with only two minute-long stoppage breaks for water. You'd be damned dehydrated by the break.' Today, a rubber lasts for three games and includes 'plenty of stoppages and time out for injury'.

In 1978, Peadar married Maureen Prendergast and took a four-year break from the sport to build their house and focus on his career with the ESB. He returned to triumph in the championships again in 1982 and 1983, retiring from the sport in the latter year, aged 40.

'The travel was a devil,' he says. 'I might have to travel from here to Kerry, Kilkenny, Kells or Croke Park to play my match. Then I'd hit the pub, as you did in those days, and have a few pints and drive home again. The county board gave you an allowance, which would just about cover your petrol, but they weren't paying for you to stay in a fancy hotel like they do now.'

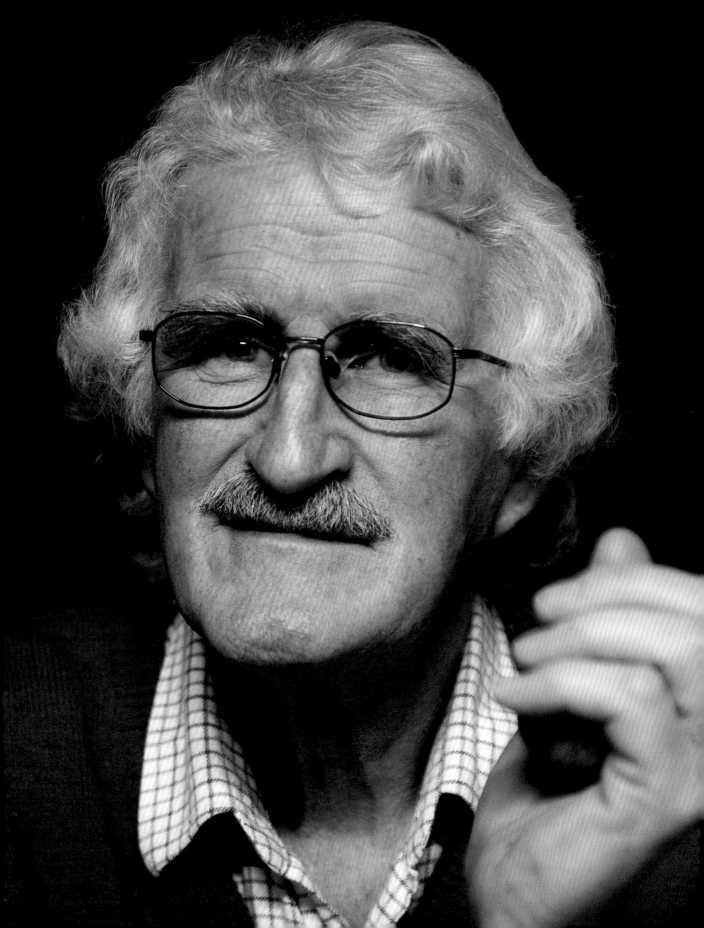

He remained with the ESB until 1989, retiring aged 46. 'The unions had come in and started computerising man days and so on. It drove me crazy, so I thought I'd pull plant and leave.'

His next venture was to borrow enough money from the bank to purchase a large catamaran, which he ran as a sea-angling boat for 12 years. *Katamara* was her name and she sailed out of Newport, escorting tourists around the islands of Clew Bay. 'It was hard work at times,' says Peadar, 'but I was always into fishing and that way of life. That's why I sell the tackle.'

Peadar retired from the Clew Bay cruises when he was 58. Today, he likes to hunt, shoot, fish and sit back amidst his fine library of books, from where he runs his modest firearms and fishing business. An annual joy is Newport's Peadar McGee International Handball Tournament, which he launched in 1980 and which still takes place every summer.

MICHAEL 'DUCKSIE' WALSH

Handball

TITLES
All-Ireland Singles: 23
All-Ireland Doubles: 15
World Masters: 2

One of the most unusual citizens of Kilkenny City during the early twentieth century was Ellen Bischoffsheim, the daughter of one of Europe's wealthiest bankers. In 1881, this Austrian Jewish heiress married the Earl of Desart and settled amid the sumptuous surroundings of Desart Court near Callan, Co. Kilkenny. In 1911, 'Countess Ellen', as she was known, became president of the Kilkenny branch of the Gaelic League. In 1922, she was appointed to the first Seanad of the Irish Free State. Her appointment stemmed from her good works in Kilkenny, and primarily the establishment of the model village of Talbot's Inch, with its woodworking and woollen industries.

One of the countess's other, less well-known legacies was the construction of the Talbot's Inch Handball Club in 1929. Indeed, the club has a sound claim to be one of the oldest, and certainly the most successful, in Ireland.

Six of Ireland's national handball champions were created upon the hallowed grounds of Talbot's Inch. However, none can hold a match to Ducksie Walsh. At the age of 44, he is able to confound most statisticians by stating that he won 38 All-Ireland titles in the space of 16 years. The way this works is in fact straightforward. Handball is played on a choice of two courts, some 60 m x 30 m, some 40 m x 20 m. There is an All-Ireland championship for both, and Ducksie has single-handedly won 23 of them. And then, of course, there is the doubles championship for both, which accounts for Ducksie's other 15 titles. He has also been a finalist in two World Handball Championships.

One of Ducksie's favourite partners has been Kilkenny hurling icon D.J. Carey, who, when not whacking sliotars through the air at Croker, is also a dab hand at handball. D.J. partnered Ducksie to three national titles. 'He never beat me, though,' smiles Ducksie, standing outside his furniture warehouse in Callan.

The Walsh family have been in Kilkenny for many aeons. Their traditional demesne is the area known as 'the Butts', set beneath the Gothic shadow of St Canice's parish church. In medieval times, this was where the Earl of Ormonde's archers practised with bows and

arrows, using mounds of earth as their targets. Ducksie's grandfather Paddy Walsh was born here in the late nineteenth century and was employed as head gardener at Newtown House, one of Kilkenny's big houses.

His other grandfather, William Burke, ran a successful drapery store in the city for years and it is through the Burkes that Ducksie discovered his passion for handball.

'I was inspired by my first cousin Billy Burke,' he says, referring to another All-Ireland handball champion from Talbot's Inch. Young Ducksie, or Michael as he was then, frequently watched his cousin play. At the age of nine, he began playing at the two corporation courts down beside St Canice's. It was winner stays on and, with money up for grabs, Ducksie quickly became utterly hooked on the sport. 'I'd be there all day Sunday,' he says, 'and I'd come home with a good few bob.'

He then started playing at the indoor courts in Talbot's Inch. At the age of ten, he won his first All-Ireland (Under-12) medal. Ducksie's hand–eye coordination caught the eye of the late coaching legend Tommy O'Brien. In 1981, O'Brien selected the 14 year old for the first Irish team to participate in the US national junior championships. The duo became close friends, and in 2001 Ducksie gave his newly won senior medal to O'Brien in appreciation of all his support.

Ducksie quickly learned that the key to success is practice. 'I trained fierce hard,' he says. 'I always have. Six days a week, from two to two and a half hours each time. If you can stick with that, it pays off.' He learned how to blast his opponents off the court with a miscellany of superb serving, exquisite passing and merciless kill shots. 'To win is the thing. I might tell my wife and friends that it's only a game at the end of the day. But if you're in the All-Ireland, you're there because you want to win.

'It's not about strength, or how fast you can get around,' he counsels. 'It's about technique. I write with my left hand and I brush my teeth with my left hand and I hit a hammer with my left hand, but I serve with my right and I made sure my right was as good as my left.'

Ducksie won his first senior All-Ireland title in 1985 when he was 18. 'And I went unbeaten for 13 years,' he says matter-of-factly. 'Then I was injured but I played anyway and I was beaten, and that was the end of that run.'

Christened Michael, he was by now much better known as Ducksie. 'A lot of Walshes in Kilkenny are called Ducksie,' he says, but he is at a loss as to why. 'My father was called Ducksie and my brothers were called Ducksie and when I started winning, they had me down as Ducksie too. And so the day I got married, even the priest called me Ducksie!'

Ducksie's father, Sean, worked as a security guard, while his mother, Vera, raised him and his seven siblings in the Butts. After he left school, Ducksie became an apprentice cabinetmaker for Bill Rafter of Deane Furniture. He then spent eight years with Paddy Sinnott before opening his own business, manufacturing and installing kitchen and bedroom interiors.

By 2001, Ducksie was struggling with alcoholism, sustaining his habit with the ritualistic drinking sessions that accompanied his every victory. One morning, he awoke to see that the man in the mirror had a very battered face. He had no memory of its cause. As the doctors stitched his chin and patched up his eyes, he accepted his predicament, checked into the Aiséirí Treatment Centre in Co. Tipperary and began following the 12 steps. Seven years later, he remains dry.

Aiséirí suggested he use his handballing skill to help his regeneration. In August 2006, he became world Over-40 champion at the Handball World Championships in Edmonton, Canada. The following year, aged 41, he earned considerable applause when he returned to contest the 2007 All-Ireland final. In 2009, he and his partner Michael Clifford narrowly missed out on a place in the All-Ireland senior doubles final. He still trains four or five nights a week, running, skipping, cycling, and is going strong at Masters level. 'One of the great things about handball is that you can keep on playing for ever.'

The game has become increasingly international and, with 16 countries on board, including Papua New Guinea and Puerto Rico, this ancient Irish sport is looking gradually more assured of a place at the Olympic Games. It undoubtedly helps that the requirements are so rudimentary – three walls, a pair of hands and a small ball is a promising start.

Ducksie has also made his mark as a fund-raiser. In 2008, he orchestrated a 72-hour handball marathon, which raised more than €50,000 for the Aislinn Adolescent Addiction Centre in Ballyragget. In 2009, he joined forces with D.J., Noel Skehan and others for a charity walk up Croagh Patrick in aid of the O'Neill Centre for cerebral palsy in Kilkenny. He has also organised a series of benefit tournaments for the Aiséirí centres.

He lives in Bennettsbridge, Co. Kilkenny, with his wife Shena and three children. His son Dylan plays handball and won the Under-15s at the US Handball Association championships in Los Angeles in 2010. 'He has it all right,' says Ducksie. 'But like every young fellow in Kilkenny he also likes to hurl.'

Michael 'Ducksie' Walsh in action against Eoin Kennedy during the 2007 All-Ireland 60 x 30 senior handball singles final at Croke Park. Kennedy emerged victorious, but Walsh's tally of 38 senior All-Ireland titles remains virtually untouchable. (© Stephen McCarthy/Sportsfile)

STEPHEN ROCHE

Cycling

MAJOR WINS
Paris–Nice 1981
Tour de Romandie 1983, 1984, 1987
Critérium International 1985
Tour de France 1987
Giro d'Italia 1987
Super Prestige Pernod International 1987

MEDALS
World Cycling Championships, 1983, bronze
World Cycling Championships, 1987, gold

It was way past midnight and Stephen Roche was still lying on his back, covered in grease and milk, trying to find the damned leak. Such, he philosophised, is the lot of a maintenance fitter. It was a general breakdown at the Merville Dairy in Finglas, Co. Dublin, where he worked. It took until 3 a.m. for someone to work it out. As the dairy creaked to life again and the employees began to file out, Stephen's boss, Ramor Craigie, approached. 'Ahm, will we see you at 9 a.m., Stephen?' he asked, a little hesitantly.

'Of course,' replied Stephen, 'but I have to cycle my 50 miles between now and then.' And such was the young man's dedication that he did. Some months later, Stephen asked the Craigies if he could have six months' leave in order to go to France to prepare for the Moscow Olympics. They gave him the six months and £500 to get started.

Born in 1959, Ireland's most successful cyclist to date was the son of Laurence Roche, an electrician's son who worked variously as a London bus driver, a Chadwick's lorry driver and a Hughes Dairy milkman. Stephen's mother, Christina Sampson, grew up on the banks of the Grand Canal in Portobello, close to the Bretzel Bakery.

Stephen recalls how his grandfather Hugh Sampson made small figurines that he sold outside Croke Park, Lansdowne Road and Glenmalure Park before the big matches. 'I used to go along every now and then and sell them with him, but we never really got to see the matches.'

Both his parents and all four of his grandparents rode bicycles. In fact, Laurence

conducted his courtship of Christina on a bicycle. 'They used to go dancing and hostelling and exploring the countryside together on bikes,' says Stephen. They married in 1957 and six children followed. Stephen was their second child.

His first ride was 'an old blue bike, which I got when I was four years old'. Shortly after this, the Roches moved from Ranelagh to Dundrum. Educated in Milltown and Dundrum, Stephen spent many a Sunday of his teenage years helping his father deliver milk so that he might raise some money for bike parts. In 1976, he became an apprentice machinist, first with Hughes Dairy and later with the Craigie brothers in Finglas.

In 1973, he joined the Orwell Wheelers Cycling Club in Dundrum. Coached by Noel O'Neill, he soon emerged as one of Ireland's leading amateurs, winning the Rás Tailteann in 1979 on a Raleigh 753 he'd purchased from Joe Daly Cycles. He was chosen to represent Ireland at the 1980 Moscow Olympics.

Stephen took his selection very seriously and decided his best form of training would be to master the French countryside. When he bade his family and colleagues adieu, few realised the 21 year old was effectively leaving Ireland for good. 'People said I'd get as far as the Eiffel Tower, go once round it, and come home again,' he laughs.

'I left for France in 1980, so I've now been living there for 30 years,' he says, a hint of the Gallic in his accent. In his first year, he joined the ACBB Boulogne-Billancourt amateur team in Paris. However, his preparations for the Olympics went skew-whiff when he picked up a knee injury shortly after winning the amateur Paris–Roubaix.

Stephen may have been dismayed that he only managed 45th place in the ensuing Olympics, but he rallied famously and used his inimitable pedalling style to win 19 races in a row upon his return to France. Peugeot were impressed and, in 1981, he turned professional and joined their cycling team. He soon had ten professional victories under his belt, including the Tour of Corsica and the Paris–Nice 'Race to the Sun'. By the close of 1983, he'd added the Tour de Romandie and the Grand Prix de Wallonie to his collection, as well as a bronze medal for Ireland at the World Cycling Championship in Switzerland.

But, of course, the biggest scalp in international cycling is the Tour de France. Stephen came thirteenth on his first attempt in 1983. Two years later, he created considerable murmurs of excitement in Ireland as he mounted the podium having come third. There was all to play for in 1986, but then Stephen crashed his bicycle at high speed during a six-day event at Paris-Bercy and bashed his right knee. He had a go at the Tour de France anyway but likened it to 'entering a dark tunnel' of pain. He squeaked home in 48th place, more than an hour and a half behind the winner.

But 1987 was to be Stephen Roche's finest year, as he secured an extraordinary litany of victories to become the world's undisputed number-one cyclist. It began when he became the first person from outside mainland Europe to win the pink jersey at the Giro d'Italia.

Then he fulfilled his childhood dream and won the Tour de France. 'I felt I'd already had a great season, so I didn't mind if I didn't win and that made me more relaxed going into it.' It was no straight run. At one point in the race, his exertions caused him to collapse and he passed out cold. Given oxygen and revived, he was asked if he was OK. He rather brilliantly replied, '*Oui, mais pas de femme tout de suite.*' ('Yes, but I'm not ready for a woman yet.')

When Roche won the contest, the Taoiseach, Charlie Haughey, seized the opportunity to join him on the podium on the Champs-Élysées. Upon his return to Dublin, the city centre

came to a standstill as more than 250,000 people paraded through the streets bedecked with Irish flags and chanting his name. He would later become the first sportsman to win Dubin's Freedom of the City.

And then, six weeks later, he pedalled home to win the World Championships in Austria. He remains one of only two cyclists to have achieved this Triple Crown, the other being the Belgian great Eddy Merckx in 1974.

For the 12 months after his victory in the Tour de France, Stephen was regularly to be seen sporting the various pink, yellow and rainbow jerseys.

However, plagued by ongoing back problems, he began to drift out of the Grand Tour cycling scene. His knee was still aching from his 1986 crash, an injury that was exacerbated when he banged it into his handlebars during the 1989 Tour de France. His back pain also led to a gradual loss of power in his left leg.

In the 1993 Tour de France, Stephen Roche came home 13th. After 13 years, with 58 professional wins to his name, he decided to call it a day.

Five years later, he moved from his home in the village of Sagy, near Paris, to the south of France where he lives today and runs the Roche Marina Hotel near Antibes. 'I was always into buildings,' he says. 'So I built a hotel. We started from scratch, renovated the whole place.' Stephen runs the show and works day and night to keep things flowing. You sense that he operates at top speed all day long. You can almost hear the wheels spinning

When he competed at the Nissan Classic in October 1986, Stephen Roche was still recovering from a crash earlier in the year in which he had damaged his right knee. In 1987, he triumphed over his injury to become one of only two cyclists who have won the Triple Crown of international cycling, namely the Tour de France, the Giro d'Italia and the UCI World Championships.
(© Ray McManus/Sportsfile)

inside him. His voice even quickens just talking about it. 'I love a challenge,' he agrees. 'When I competed, I loved the challenge. I work better when I have something to go to. I'm probably obsessed by it but I don't have any problem sleeping. I can go on four hours' sleep. But once I sit down and stop, I close my eyes and I'm gone.'

'I do still try to find time to cycle whenever I can and I run a bit, an hour here, an hour there, to keep me in training. I ran the New York marathon in 2008 and the Birmingham half-marathon in 2009.' Stephen is patron of the annual Tour de Cure cycling event in Midleton, Co. Cork, which raises money for cancer care, persons with intellectual disability and the Irish Anaphylaxis Campaign. He's also had a crack at riding pretty much every type of bike that is going. He was fine on a penny-farthing and he's stayed afloat on circus bikes, which have crossbars and wheels and springs and saddles shooting out in all the wrong directions. 'The only one I didn't get any mileage out of was a one-wheeler, a unicycle, but I once met Patrick Dempsey, the actor, and he got up and rode one no problem. It's all a question of balance.'

Stephen's son, 26-year-old Nicolas, led the AG2R La Mondiale team at the 2010 Tour de France. Nicolas's cousin Daniel Martin is also one of Ireland's leading cyclists and was the country's 2008 road champion.

KEN DOHERTY

Snooker

It was 'Winner Stays On' at Jason's in Ranelagh and the kid just could not be beat. Men and women of every shape, size and sexual persuasion grabbed the cue and tried their damnedest. But even when they landed the white in the sneakiest of places, the boy would somehow figure a way around it. If it is any consolation to those who failed, the kid was Ken Doherty and he was already on a course that would see him become champion of Ireland, world junior champion, world amateur champion and, come 1997, straight-up world champion.

Jason's was undoubtedly the making of his star. Ken was eight years old when the south Dublin snooker hall opened in 1976. He already had a pocket-sized snooker table, a Christmas present from his father, upon which he played religiously. Henceforth, every Sunday afternoon, Ken headed down to Jason's with his big brother, bypassed the jukeboxes and pinball machines and made a beeline for the snooker table. 'They got me a biscuit tin to stand on while I played,' he recalls. 'Sure, I was only a baby!'

His passion for snooker was further ignited in 1982 when he tuned in to watch Alex Higgins win the world championship. 'That was one of the best moments in sport,' says Ken. 'The wife came out with the baby and he takes the baby in one arm and the cup in the other. Higgins inspired a lot of people to watch and play snooker. I was one of them.'

Within a year of Higgins's victory, 13-year-old Ken was mourning the death of his father, Tony Doherty. The event would bring him considerably closer to his two older

brothers, Seamus and Anthony, and the Doherty boys grew up quick.

The Doherty family originated in Co. Donegal but had settled in Dublin by the early twentieth century, when Ken's great-grandfather Patrick worked as a fishmonger. Ken's grandfather, also Patrick, ran a bookmaker's office on Baggot Street. When the bookie's went belly up following a victory by the favourite in the Grand National, Patrick went to work for a blood bank. Patrick's funeral was a well attended affair and he was buried in St Mary's Church on Haddington Road, where there is a war memorial recalling his older brother Jack, a private in the Dublin Fusiliers, who was killed in action in Belgium in 1915.

Born in 1924, Ken's father, Tony, was the eldest of Patrick's three sons and the only one who married. He met Ken's mother, Rose Lawler, while working as a houseman with the Marist Fathers at the Catholic University School on Leeson Street, where she was the cook. Tony later found work as a night porter at the Royal Exchange Hotel on Parliament Street. In time, he and Rose moved to Trinity Hall by Palmerston Park, where he worked as the porter and she as a cook. 'They were very hard times,' says Ken. 'They lived in half a house with another family below them. I remember my mother would take in a blind woman for a six-week holiday every year.'

Rose was the daughter of James Lawler, a cabinetmaker from Bawnogues on Baltinglass Hill, Co. Wicklow. The house is still in the family and Ken has climbed the hill many a time. 'I nearly died in Baltinglass,' he says. He was messing about with his brother and cousin. They pretended to throw money into a slurry pit and six-year-old Ken stumbled in after it. 'It was like quicksand. Next thing I'm down to my knees and seconds later I'm up to my neck.' Fortunately, his cousin grasped him in the nick of time. 'My uncle came down on his bicycle and carried me through the town. I had three Dettol baths to get rid of the stench.'

When Ken was born in 1968, the family lived at Swan Place, just off Morehampton Road. Three years later, they moved to Ranelagh Avenue. All three Doherty brothers went to the Christian Brothers School on Westland Row. 'It was a real nice school,' says Ken. 'Tough and in a tough area, but thankfully we never witnessed any trouble from the Brothers.' As a sign of his appreciation, he later gifted the school two snooker tables and he presents the trophy to their annual tournament winner.

Three months after his father's death, 'the guys at Jason's started to give me free practice, an hour a day'. Ken attended every day. 'You grow up very quickly in a place like that because you're with adults all the time.' He showed his gratitude to Jason's by shaking the Irish snooker world upside down later that same year.

First, he narrowly lost in the finals of the *Evening Herald* Under-16 championships. Then he entered the Irish Under-16s and 'beat the guy who'd beaten me to win the whole thing'. With the approval of his school principal, Brother Paul Hendrick, he began taking more and more time off to compete. He secured his place on the Irish team, initially as an Under-16 and then, from the age of 14, as a senior.

At the age of 18, Ken completed his Leaving Certificate, moved to England and began his global conquest. In 1989, he became Irish amateur champion. He went on to win the world amateur title that same year. He turned pro in 1991, losing 10–8 to Steve Davis in the televised stages of that year's world championship.

His 18–12 victory over Stephen Hendry at the Crucible in the 1997 world championship final was an epic. 'The world professional was the pinnacle,' he says. 'That's what you dream of.' More than 250,000 people lined the streets of Dublin to welcome Ireland's first

world snooker champion home. A further 60,000 roared their approval when he paraded his trophy on the pitch at Old Trafford, where his beloved Manchester United play. The event was all the more poignant for the fact that he was only 12 years old when he chose the warped cue he used to beat Hendry. He was so on fire that year that he also secured a Guinness world record, potting all the colours in sequence in 23.4 seconds.

In 1998, the reigning world champion returned to Ranelagh, where he lives today with his wife, Sarah, their small son, Christian, and a pair of King Charles black and tans. His home is entirely free of sporting memorabilia. That is all kept in his own private snooker den at the Radisson Hotel in Stillorgan, a consolation prize from the Cosgraves, owners of both the hotel and Jason's, when they made the lamented decision to close the snooker hall down. This is the space where Ken practises today, on a Riley table just like the one he became world champ on back in 1997. You sense that he misses the live banter of Jason's, the one-liners that made him erupt with a deep rumbling laugh, not unlike Boycie from *Only Fools and Horses*. But all that is an age ago now.

Ken's den is not without its humorous moments. A few months after George Best died, Alex Higgins popped in for a practice. Ken pointed at a photo of himself standing beside the great Belfast footballer and said, 'There's an old friend of yours.' Alex approached the photo, took off his glasses and regarded it intently. 'Oh, yes,' he said, at length. 'Georgie Best . . . what a waste.'

Ken Doherty in action during his second-round victory over Thailand's James Wattana in the 2006 Northern Ireland Trophy at the Waterfront Hall in Belfast. The Dubliner was provisional world number one for much of the 2006—07 season.
(© Oliver McVeigh/Sportsfile)

Despite all the cities and landscapes he has visited, Ken's preferred holiday destination is Ireland, primarily Killarney or Connemara. 'There's no place like it,' he says. 'We always give out about the Irish weather but I don't like hot weather. When it's too hot I get freckles and go pink and I have to slap on suncream all the time. I can't lie around on a beach or by a pool all day. Pink isn't a good colour!'

Pale he may be, but Ken enjoys the outdoor life and keeps fit playing golf and soccer. He is also increasingly adept at poker and has played in the last two Irish Opens. 'I love the buzz of poker,' he grins. 'The gamble, the chance . . . it's one of the few buzzes I get that's on a par with a snooker tournament. It's a lot like snooker. You have to be focused and stay cool under pressure. You have to be passive, you have to be aggressive. There's a lot of body language, a lot of psychology and, unlike snooker, where there are too many gentlemen, there's a lot of yapping.'

Between 1997 and 2003, Ken spent 15 years in the world's top 16, reaching the world championship finals in 1997, 1998 and 2003. At the close of the 2005–06 season, he was ranked as the world number two. He continues to compete, going out in the first round of the 2010 world championship to Mark Selby. He has also proven himself a useful analyst, which may stand him in good favour with the BBC. Ken remains the only snooker player ever to have been both world amateur and world professional champion.

DES SMYTH

Golf

MAJOR WINS
Amateur
West of Ireland Amateur Open
 Championship, 1968

Professional
European Tour: 8
Champions Tour: 2
European Seniors Tour: 2
Other: 8

TEAM APPEARANCES
Hennessy Cognac Cup: 3 (2 wins, 1980,
 1982)
Alfred Dunhill Cup: 5 (1 win, 1988)
Ryder Cup: 2
World Cup: 5
UBS Cup: 1

'What's great about golf is that you can start when you are four years old and you can play for ever. You don't get injured and it keeps you active. I've got friends of 80 years of age who jump out of bed in the morning to play a round. And they are marching! That's living proof that there's a long life after 40.'

So says Desmond John Smyth, champion golfer and Ryder Cup veteran, who was born in the port town of Drogheda, Co. Louth, on 12 February 1953. His grandfather and father were in the victualler trade, running a butcher's and slaughter yard in Drogheda.

Des is the third of four sons, all of whom developed a passion for the game. The origin of their fervour is not complex. They grew up in the village of Bettystown, less than one mile from the windswept links course of the Laytown and Bettystown Golf Club on the coast of Co. Meath.

'That whole coastal area is something of a golfing Mecca,' says Des. 'The golf club was very strong on promoting junior players and it became a sort of golfing nursery. My brothers and I all played football and tennis, but golf was the only sport you could play on your own. We started on the beach and we slowly graduated to the club. I happened to be good at it and I started winning junior competitions, which boosted my ego and inspired me to practise more.'

During the mid-1960s, Des represented his club in contests against rivals such as Co. Louth, Malahide and Royal Dublin. In 1968, he won the West of Ireland Amateur Open Championship at Rosses Point, Co. Sligo. He also won 'a couple of scratch cups'. At

the age of 16, Des also played for his school, St Joseph's Christian Brothers School in Drogheda, when they won the inaugural Irish Schools Match Play Championships. The Leinster selectors duly took note of the youngster and picked him for their junior team in the provincial championships. By the age of 18, Des was playing at senior level for Ireland.

He was scheduled to represent Ireland in the Walker Cup – the amateur version of the Ryder Cup – when he was injured in a car accident. As his wounded shoulder recovered, he was faced with a critical decision: remain an amateur and have another crack at the Walker Cup in two years' time, or bite the bullet and become a tournament professional, a golf pro.

He turned pro in 1974, shortly after his 20th birthday. 'I'd always wanted to be a professional golfer,' he says. 'I loved the idea of making a living playing golf. So now it was all about the prize money and I was looking to see what tours I could join.' It wasn't an easy transition. 'I had a rough ride because I just wasn't strong enough to begin with, and I struggled for four or five years.'

The butcher's son from Co. Louth served his time in countries such as Kenya, Nigeria and Zambia. 'They were pretty tough places to be 37 years ago,' he says. 'They were small tournaments and you funded yourself, so when you won, you reinvested it. If you stuck it out, you became a better player. But it's a hard world and a lot of guys came and went. You only read about those on top. You don't hear about the ones who fall out the sides. There were times when I thought, I'm not going to make it.'

In 1979, he had his European Tour breakthrough, winning the Sun Alliance European Match Play Championship. 'That broke the ice for me,' he says. 'That gave me the confidence I'd been missing. Confidence is such a big part of the game. Everyone hits a dip, so it's all about finding a way to improve, or cope, or move onwards.' He went on to win the first of his six Irish National PGA Championships that summer and played on the European team for the 1979 Ryder Cup.

For nearly forty years, he has played in tournaments all over the world, spending approximately nine months a year on the road. From May to September, he joined the European Tour, and otherwise he was often in South Africa or Australia. He also did six years on the Champions Tour in America. He was on the Ryder Cup team again in 1981, and played in five World Cups. In 1988, he partnered Eamonn Darcy and Ronan Rafferty to win the Alfred Dunhill Cup at St Andrews, and he personally finished seventh on the 1988 European Tour's Order of Merit.

In 2001, Des used his signature long 'broomhandle' putter to great effect to become the oldest man to win a European Tour event, claiming the Madeira Island Open at the age of 48 years and 34 days. Two years later, he became the first European to win the US Senior Tour qualifying school outright, scooping prize money of close to $1 million in his first season. He was one of Ian Woosnam's vice captains at the 2006 Ryder Cup, which took place at The K Club in Co. Kildare. He also won both the 2005 Arcapita Seniors Tour Championship and the 2007 Wentworth Senior Masters.

'I always thought that there would come a point where I wasn't making that much money, because there's young guys coming in all the time. But it didn't happen. The game grew, the TV companies got interested and then Sky got involved, because they have a TV on every wall of every hotel, pub and club. So a lot more money came into

the game, which meant that, while I was definitely working harder, I could keep making money.'

He continues to play on the European Senior Tour during the summer. 'Basically, every tournament lasts a week,' he says. 'You get out on a Tuesday and you're out there until Sunday, all day, every day.' He has also turned his hand to course design, most notably with what is considered to be a cracking links course at Seapoint near Termonfeckin in Co. Louth.

'We have a great golfing history in this country,' he says. 'It's one of those sports where Ireland punches well above its weight. We're a tiny country, yet we keep producing golfers who are hitting the top ten in the world. There's 30 million golfers in America!' He reckons Rory McIlroy is 'the best we've ever seen. He is the real deal and he's going to be our Tiger Woods.'

'I'm 57 and I'm going to play the European Senior Tour for a few years yet,' he says. 'I've always enjoyed what I'm doing. I feel very fortunate because when I started at 20, I thought, if I get 20 years out of this and enjoy it and make a few bucks, that would be great. The way life has gone, I'm nearly 40 years at it and I'm still making a few quid. I know it's near the end. In golfing terms, I'm way down the back nine in my career! But I've enjoyed the ride.'

Des Smyth watches his drive from the third tee at the 1998 Irish PGA Golf Championship in Powerscourt, Co. Wicklow. The gentleman golfer from Co. Louth won the contest in 1996 and 2001, during a career that saw him rack up eight European Tour wins. (© Matt Brown/Sportsfile)

MAEVE KYLE

Athletics and Hockey

Athletics

ACHIEVEMENTS

Olympics
1956, 100 m, 200 m
1960, 100 m, 200 m
1964, 400 m, semi-final; 800m, semi-final

European Indoor Championships
1966, 400 m, bronze

British Championships
1961, 400 m, gold

AWARDS
World All-Star Hockey Team, 1953, 1959
Ulster Athletic Association Hall of Fame, 2005
Lifetime Achievement Award, Coaching Awards, 2006
Irish Hockey Hall of Fame, 2006
OBE, 2008
RTÉ/Irish Sports Council Hall of Fame, 2008
Trinity College Sports Hall of Fame, 2010

Hockey

CAPS
Ireland: 58

'I was a disgrace to motherhood and the Irish nation,' says Maeve Kyle proudly. 'That's what one letter in the *Irish Times* said. Imagine! A woman leaving her husband and daughter to go and run!'

The letter she refers to was written in 1956, shortly after the Kilkenny athlete was selected to represent Ireland in the women's 100 m and 200 m at the Olympic Games in Melbourne. Catholic Ireland was not quite ready for women athletes. 'We weren't any different to some of the Islamic countries today, really,' says Maeve. 'We didn't have to cover our heads, but we weren't to run in an unseemly manner and they certainly didn't want us showing any leg.'

Maeve grew up along the banks of the River Nore in Kilkenny City. 'The river was our playground,' she says. 'My older brothers and I were always down there, jumping in

off the steps, running through the woods, fishing for eels and swimming with the otters. Nobody ever asked us where we went or what devilment we were up to. As long as you arrived home for lunch, you were fine.'

Home was Kilkenny College, the illustrious seat of learning founded in the reign of Henry VIII to which her father had been appointed headmaster in 1917. Carrodus Gilbert Shankey was an intellectual with an engineer's mind, descended from a family of 'wanderers and adventurers'. He remained headmaster for the next 35 years. In 1927, he married Enid Thrift and their daughter Maeve was born in Kilkenny the following year.

'Daddy was quite austere and autocratic,' says Maeve. 'My mother was the mad one. She was a natural science gold medallist. One time, the college governors came for lunch and my mother was nowhere to be seen. Daddy sent a maid to find her and eventually she came back: "She's up a chestnut tree, sir, looking at a pigeon's nest. She says she'll be down shortly."

'Sport was part of my social life growing up. It didn't cost you anything. It couldn't, because we had no money!' Gaelic games also appealed. 'Young Protestant children didn't generally get an opportunity to play Gaelic games,' she says, 'but Daddy would let the boys have a go at hurling and I played handball in a covered alley at the college.'

In 1937, Maeve's grandfather W.E. Thrift became provost of Trinity College Dublin. Maeve, at school in Alexandra College, moved in with her grandparents, where she enjoyed unusual company at the Provost's House. Her grandfather was a chess grandmaster and one of his regular opponents was Éamon de Valera.

Maeve was first and foremost a hockey player. Having mastered the sport at school, she went on to win 58 Irish caps, as well as representing the South-East (alongside her mother), Leinster and Ulster at different stages of her career. She was named in the World All-Star team in 1953 and 1959.

In 1953, she was selected for the Irish squad to compete at the World Conference in Folkestone. At a post-match party in Antrim, she was introduced to Mr Sean Kyle of Ballymena. At length, Sean offered her two things. First, he would ensure she was fit enough for the Folkestone games. Second, when training was well under way, he asked her to marry him. They were wed in February 1954.

'You never know what's around the corner,' laughs Maeve, 'but isn't that just as well? I met the fellow on a blind date and married him and I've never been back since. When you move from one rural parish to another, you stand out like a white blackbird, but I've made it my home up here now.'

In 1955, Maeve and Sean co-founded the Ballymena and Antrim Athletic Club. It was originally designed as a women's club, but within a year they had men on board too. The club continues to thrive to the present day, and in 2008 it won the coveted UK Athletic Club of the Year award.

Meanwhile, Sean taught Maeve how to run. In 1956, the 28 year old went to Melbourne to compete in the 100 m and 200 m. 'My biggest claim to fame is that I was the first Irish woman to go to the Olympics. You could call me an athletic suffragette, I suppose. Young married women just didn't go running in foreign lands. They didn't feed me to the lions, but I'm sure some of them would have wanted to!'

To get to Australia, Maeve and Sean had to raise £200, a huge sum but par for the course for athletes of that era. The journey took more than two weeks, with stop-offs in New York, San Francisco (where they scooped up Ronnie Delany) and Fiji, before arriving in Melbourne to an amazing reception from Australia's massive Irish expat community.

The Irish team returned home with five medals, including Delany's 1,500 m gold. Maeve ran in the 200 m because that was the farthest a woman was allowed to run in 1956. 'They felt we would require resuscitation if we ran any further,' she chuckles.

She subsequently competed in the 1960 Rome Olympics, but 'I just wasn't fast enough on the sprints'. At this time, the Olympic Council introduced two new distances for women, the 400 m and the 800 m. 'To me, the 400 is the greatest event of the lot. You have to stay in your own lane. You've got to think. You can't sprint the whole way. You've got to judge and you've got to not be influenced by the people either side of you. Those are all serious challenges, both mentally and physically.

'I said to Sean, I'm going to try the 400. And he said, "Oh, good girl." I thought, you swine, you don't believe I can! I told him I was going to win the British Championships and he still didn't believe me. I never for one minute believed I wasn't going to win. That is the only time in my life I have ever been in that situation. So I finished and I won it, and it was a new British record. I always knew I would win it. That's when I learned about the power of the mind over the body and decided to go back and study sports psychology. None of us understand how powerful the mind is. If you really make up your mind that something will happen, then it can happen. It is actually quite scary. You have to be ready for it.'

Former Olympian Maeve Kyle judges Claire McNamara of Athenry AC during the senior women's pole vault event at the Woodie's DIY 2010 Senior Indoor Championships in Belfast. (© Stephen McCarthy/ Sportsfile)

Maeve's victory made her the first Irish female to triumph in the British track championships. Her time of 54.3 was also a new British record and she was now among the fastest 400 m runners in the world. In 1964, aged 36, she went to Tokyo to represent Ireland at her third Olympic Games. She reached the semi-finals of both the 400 m and 800 m. Two years later, she took bronze in the 400 m at the European Indoor Athletics Championships in Dortmund.

'I loved the 400, but it just came in too late for me,' she says philosophically. 'You can't relive the past and you can't really do much about tomorrow except prepare for something you think may happen. And then it may not happen like you thought it would! Sometimes it's a good job that we don't know what tomorrow will bring!'

In the subsequent decades, she and Sean concentrated on developing their award-winning club. When all else was gloom in the 1970s, the Kyles' club was instrumental in maintaining links between Northern Ireland's various towns through the celebrated Rotary Club-sponsored Top Towns meetings. Maeve is also chairwoman of Coaching NI.

DR RONNIE DELANY

Athletics

ACHIEVEMENTS
Olympics
1956, 1,500 m, gold
1960, 800 m, 1,500 m

European Championships
1958, 1,500 m, bronze

World University Games
1961, 800 m, gold

AWARDS
Texaco Sportstars Award, 1959
Chairman of the Irish Sports Council (1978–90)
Texaco Sportstars Hall of Fame, 1982
Freedom of the City of Dublin, 2006
Honorary Doctor of Laws, University College Dublin, 2006
Honorary Fellowship, Royal College of Surgeons in Ireland
President, Irish Olympians Association
President, Irish Chapter Villanova Alumni Association

TITLES
Irish: 4
Amateur Athletic Union (USA): 4
National Collegiate Athletic Association
  (USA): 4

In the decade before JFK got shot and Neil and Buzz strolled upon the moon, for the Irish there was only one defining 'where were you when it happened?' moment. And that was all about the warm, still December afternoon in 1956 when Ronnie Delany, 'the man from Eire', crossed the finishing line at the Melbourne Olympics to win the 1,500 m and give Ireland its first gold medal in 24 years.

The Wicklow-born student's victory over the world's best runners was a huge boost for Ireland at a time when emigration was running rampant and the economy was through the floor.

Regarded as an outside chance, Ronnie didn't just beat his 11 rivals, he surged forward from 10th position at the bell to annihilate them in the last 400 m, finishing in a record-breaking

3:41.2. For the 110,000 people who watched him in the stadium, it was a veritable epic.

Earlier that year, the twenty-one-year-old Irishman had become only the seventh man – and the youngest of them all – to run a mile in under four minutes, clocking 3:59.0 in Compton, California.

Ronnie was born in Arklow in 1935. His father, Patrick Antonius Delany, known as 'P.A.', was a customs and excise officer. 'The Delanys were dynastic farmers from Batterstown in Co. Meath,' says Ronnie. 'They still farm the same land today.' Three of his uncles stayed on the land. Ronnie was a frequent visitor to their homes during his childhood. 'Oh, yes, I was fed on good fresh country eggs from Meath.'

Ronnie's mother, Brigid, was a nurse, as well as a qualified 'cap and gown' piano and violin teacher. Her father, Joe Hughes, was a Wexford-born publican and grocer who ran the premises now occupied by O'Brien's pub on Leeson Street. 'I slept in that pub until I was ten or eleven years old,' says Ronnie.

Shortly after the start of the Second World War, P.A. was transferred to Dublin and the family relocated to Sandymount. This was where Ronnie grew up, playing tennis, hockey, cricket and lawn bowls with his brothers, listening to boxing matches on the wireless with his father.

As a teenager, Ronnie advanced from O'Connell's Christian Brothers School in North Richmond Street to the Catholic University School on Leeson Street. Ronnie and his elder brother Joe would often race each other home from school. 'Unknowingly, I was "putting in the mileage", in running parlance, developing my leg strength and cardiovascular system.'

At the age of 17, Ronnie ran – and won – his first big race with an 880-yard sprint at the Leinster Colleges Championships. The experience confirmed his faith that he could win. 'In a perverse way I enjoyed the nervousness of competing and the butterflies in the tummy that went with it.'

Towards the end of his school days, he was preparing to race. 'Father, will I have a go at the record?' he asked the athletic coach. Father Lonergan replied, 'Ronnie, don't do anything of the sort. Run to win your race.' Ronnie followed that advice ever after.

By the end of 1953, he was an All-Ireland champion and a bright athletic prospect at both the half-mile and the mile. The following year, he went to the European Championships in Berne and reached the final of the 800 m. His performance helped win him a scholarship to Villanova University in Pennsylvania, an athletics hothouse. Ronnie studied economics, and later dabbled in the theatre. 'I was an appalling producer. And I was an even worse actor. I played Colonel Pickering and I was truly awful.'

Fortunately, acting wasn't why he had gone to America. Ronnie trained and Ronnie ran. Coached by the great Jumbo Elliott, he became known as 'the Villanova Rocket'.

'I ran indoors for five years in America without losing. I remember an article they did at the time called "Is the US a Second Class Sporting Nation?" They wrote it because there was this mad Irishman who kept beating them all the time!'

Between 1956 and 1959, Ronnie won an unprecedented 40 straight victories on the 'indoors' tracks in America, including the Wanamaker Mile at Madison Square Garden, breaking the world indoor mile record three times. He also became known for 'Delany's Doubles', where he won both the half-mile and the mile, or the 1,000 yards and the two mile, at the same event.

Then there was the small matter of an Olympic gold, which he picked up in 1956, followed by a bronze medal won at the 1958 European Championships.

Ronnie represented Ireland in the 800 m at the 1960 Olympics, but an injury to his Achilles' tendon knocked him out at the quarter-final stage. The following year, he recovered his strength to become Ireland's first gold medallist at the World University Games, winning the 800 m in Sofia, Bulgaria.

In Ireland, he was – and, to an extent, still is – cheered wherever he went. It was little different in the USA. His face was splashed all over the cover of *Sports Illustrated* and every other newspaper and magazine. 'A young kid comes to America, makes good. My name was a lead story. I was in the papers all the time. Being a huge brand name in America, everyone wants you. I got offered things like to play the part of a cop in a Broadway musical. They thought my story was a romantic one.'

And then, in 1962, the 26 year old announced his retirement from competitive athletics, citing recurring problems in his Achilles tendon. On the same day, he announced his engagement to Joan Riordan, who became the mother of his four children.

'One of my proudest moments was when my son said to me, later in my life, "Dad, I never knew that you were a famous sportsperson until I was about ten years of age." I thought that was beautiful. To him I was just Dad. I wasn't Ronnie Delany, the iconic athlete.'

The Delanys live in Carrickmines and are frequently visited by their children and 14 grandchildren. 'They are very keen and ambitious. I try and explain to them that they must never be worried about losing. I never had a problem about losing.'

Ronnie is not just an icon because he won the gold. It's also because of the follow-up, his immense contribution to Irish sport in the decades since he won, all conducted with an old-fashioned roguish Dublin charm, spliced with his intimate knowledge of the

At the 1956 Olympics in Melbourne, Ronnie Delany created one of the biggest upsets in the history of the track when he broke free of the opposition to cruise home a clear gold-medal winner in the 1,500 m. (© IOC/Allsport, Getty Images)

international sporting world. That is why he has received an honorary doctorate from University College Dublin and an honorary fellowship from the Royal College of Surgeons. That is why he was for many years the chairman of the Irish Sports Council and is today the president of the Irish Olympians Association. That is why there is a huge portrait of him by James Hanley in the National Portrait Gallery. That is why he got the Freedom of the City of Dublin. That is why his face has appeared on postage stamps from Ireland to the Dominican Republic and North Korea. And that is why, more than 40 years after the 1956 Olympics took place, the Irish public voted him Champion of Champions.

EAMONN COGHLAN

Athletics

ACHIEVEMENTS

Olympics
1976, 1,500 m, 4th
1980, 5,000 m, 4th
1988, 5,000 m

World Championships
1983, 5,000 m, gold

IAAF World Cup
1981, 5,000 m, 1st

European Indoor Championships
1979, 1,500 m, gold

European Outdoor Championships
1978, 1,500 m, silver

Millrose Games (Wanamaker Mile, New York)
7-time champion, 1977–87

AWARDS
Texaco Sportstars Hall of Fame, 2006
Grand Marshal of Dublin's St Patrick's Day Parade, 2008

In the history of this planet, only one person over forty years of age has managed to run the mile in less than four minutes. In fact, Eamonn Coghlan was 41 when he clocked 3:58.15 on the track at Harvard University. For a man who has run the mile in less than four minutes on eighty-three occasions, that particular one was a stand-out. But while Eamonn is justly acclaimed for his prowess at the mile – he held the world indoor record for the mile for 18 years – he has also excelled at the 1,500 m and the 5,000 m.

Patrick Coghlan, Eamonn's grandfather, was a printer's assistant from South Dock Street, off Shelbourne Road, in Dublin. Patrick died from a stroke at the age of thirty-four in 1922, leaving his widow Kitty with three small children, William Aloysius (known as Bill), Cora and Patrick, who died of tuberculosis in his infancy. Kitty returned to the Breen family home on South William Street where she had grown up.

The Breens were a staunchly Catholic family and the youngsters were obliged to attend mass at St Teresa's on Clarendon Street every day. Under his mother's careful supervision, young Bill became an altar boy. In 1947, he married Catherine King, a ladies' blouse-maker,

who lived just off Bath Avenue in Dublin 4. They moved to Cooley Road in Drimnagh, where they had five children.

Eamonn, their fourth child, was born in 1952. He enjoyed a happy childhood, often in cahoots with his best friend and soulmate, Brian Kerr, who went on to manage the Irish soccer team. 'He was managing street leagues when we were kids,' laughs Eamonn. They were energetic boys and lapped up every sport they could: 'Gaelic football, hurling, soccer, cricket – you name it.'

Eamonn played soccer for Rialto until he was 13. But he had also begun to take an interest in running. He learned the benefits of speed when, as a youngster puffing cigarettes and kicking a ball about on 'the field' in Drimnagh, 'the toughs from Crumlin came over with hurling sticks looking for trouble . . . I was no hero. I ran.' At any rate, when the Rialto soccer timetable clashed with Sunday athletics, Eamonn chose athletics.

His interest in athletics was inspired by his father, Bill Coghlan, who became president of the Athletics Association of Ireland in 1979. Indeed, Eamonn's broader introduction to the possibilities of sport came through his father's work at Breen Electrical. Established by Eamonn's great-uncle Louis, Breen's was perhaps the best-known electrical contracting company in Ireland during the 1950s and 1960s. Amongst many contracts, they looked after the sound for matches at Croke Park and the former Shamrock Rovers stadium at Glenmalure Park. Bill Coghlan was a key player in the business and his young son was never far behind.

'Electrics was my passion as a kid,' says Eamonn. 'Had I not been so successful in athletics, I would have become an electrician. And to this day, I sometimes get frustrated that I didn't gain my apprenticeship. It would have been so natural to me. I went on as many jobs with my father as I could, putting up the wires and setting up the sound system. And every weekend I'd go to Croke Park or watch the Rovers.'

From the age of 13, Eamonn was educated amid the red bricks and frog-filled waters of the Christian Brothers School in Drimnagh Castle. He joined a group of athletes in Celtic Athletics Club. And when the Celtic broke up, he joined Metropolitan Harriers, who became arguably the best junior running club in the country.

'We were all as good as one another really,' says Eamonn, who won the Leinster colleges' 5,000 m title in 1970. 'And yet I am the only one of that group of Under-14 champions who pursued a career in athletics. There was an element of luck there, for sure, but I found out that I loved running. It became an expression of myself.'

His confidence was considerably boosted when he came into contact with his new coach Gerry Farnan. 'Gerry saw something in me that he believed in and he instilled that self-belief back into me.' In 1971, following victories in the All-Ireland 1,500 m and 5,000 m titles, Coghlan was offered a scholarship at Villanova University, a private university just outside Philadelphia that specialises in training athletes to Olympic standards.

Over the next four years, he was coached by the legendary Jumbo Elliott, under whom he ran his first four-minute mile in Pittsburgh, before breaking the long-standing European outdoor mile record. He also won four National Collegiate Athletic Association (NCAA) individual titles.

Upon his graduation in 1976, he went to the Montreal Olympics and competed in the 1,500 m, finishing fourth. A commentator remarked, 'He may not have won, but, by God, for four minutes he united Ireland.'

'My running mantra is to relax, relax. A huge amount of adrenalin flows during the days before a race. You try to switch off because you want to save your emotional energy for the race. Once the gun goes, you're in the zone. Sometimes the negative thoughts are still there and you're thinking, I wish I could trip on the side of the kerb and get the hell out. But no, you switch them off and focus, focus, constantly focus, on staying relaxed, holding your position and waiting to make the right move. It happens very quickly in a four-minute race.'

Eamonn's trademark 'move' was his kick and acceleration manoeuvre, made all the more memorable when Adidas tailor-made his shoes, which were 'green for Ireland and stuck out a mile'. In 1979, he used his kick to stunning effect, winning a much coveted gold at the European Indoor Championships in Vienna. He returned to a hero's welcome at Dublin Airport. His homecoming was immortalised on film when he placed the gold medal around the neck of his newborn daughter Suzanne.

Eamonn's favourite event was probably the Wanamaker Mile, an indoor one-mile race held annually in New York City's Madison Square Garden and a traditional magnet for Irish runners. Eamonn echoed Ronnie Delany's triple victory of 1956–59 and went on to trump it with a record-breaking seven triumphs between 1977 and 1987. As the track surface was made of wood, wags christened him 'Chairman of the Boards'. Eamonn's Wanamaker record stood for twenty-three years before Kenyan-born athlete Bernard Lagat won the race an eighth time at the 2010 Millrose Games. Eamonn fired the pistol at the record-breaking race.

Eamonn Coghlan sets the pace in the 1,500 m at the 1986 National Championships in Tullamore, six weeks ahead of the European Championships in Stuttgart. In 1994, the Dubliner clocked the mile at 3:58.15, making him the first man in the world aged 40 or older to run the mile in less than 4 minutes. (© Ray McManus/Sportsfile)

In 1983, Eamonn bounced back from a career-threatening injury to win gold in the 5,000 m at the inaugural 1983 World Championships in Helsinki. This was the race in which he famously clenched a triumphant fist more than 100 m from the finish line, knowing he had won. He also bettered his own indoor mile world record to 3:49.78, which remains the second-fastest indoor mile of all time.

Following his graduation from Villanova in 1976, Eamonn married Yvonne Murphy, his childhood sweetheart. They settled in the USA for 19 years, initially in San Diego and later in Rye, New York. Eamonn came back to Ireland every summer to compete on the European track circuit. In 1990, the Coghlans returned to Dublin for good and built their present house in Porterstown. 'In America, it's so easy to forget your roots and we really wanted our kids to know that Ireland was where they were from,' says Eamonn.

In 1994, the forty-one year old secured his place in athletics annals with his masters sub-four-minute mile. Since hanging up his spikes, he has been increasingly busy at home and abroad. He is a member of the board of the Irish Sports Council and a director of the Children's Medical and Research Foundation in Our Lady's Children's Hospital in Crumlin. He is a regular panellist on RTÉ for athletics programmes. He does a lot of public speaking and motivational talks. He coaches Irish international runners with aspirations to compete in the London and Rio Olympic Games. Eamonn continues to jog regularly but says, 'I need carrots in front of me or else I'll lose interest.' He has run four marathons, the fastest in 2:24.15 in New York, and a fifth is probably in the offing.

SONIA O'SULLIVAN

Athletics

ACHIEVEMENTS

Olympics
2000, 5,000 m, silver

World Championships
1993, 1,500 m, silver
1995, 5,000 m, gold

European Championships
1994, 3,000 m, gold
1998, 5,000 m, gold; 10,000 m, gold
2002, 5,000 m, silver; 10,000 m, silver

World Cross-Country Championships
1997, team 8 km, bronze
1998, 4 km, gold; 8 km, gold
2002, team 4 km, bronze

World Indoor Championships
1997, 3,000 m, silver

AWARDS
Texaco Sportstars Award, 1992, 1993, 1994, 1995, 2000, 2002,
Texaco Special Achievement Award, 1993
European Athlete of the Year, 1995
RTÉ Sportsperson of the Year, 2000
ESB/Rehab People of the Year, Greatest Living Sportsperson 2004

It is just over 17,000 km from Sonia O'Sullivan's adopted home in Melbourne, Australia, to the hotel in Howth, Co. Dublin, where we meet. Trundling up the rain-swept drive to meet her, I do some idle calculations; 17,000 km divided by 5,000 m, Sonia's favourite running distance. So that means Sonia would have to run her favourite distance 3,400 times to get from here to Melbourne. And then I get to thinking, I bet she's run 5,000 m at least 3,400 times. I mean, she runs twice that distance every day just to stay in shape. My goodness, this dame has run all the way from Dublin to Australia. And probably back again too.

But on this occasion she has journeyed by plane. She's back in Ireland for a few weeks, to keep an eye on what Europe has in store for the athletes of the world this summer. The moment her plane touched down, she slipped into her runners and went for a jog.

'Whenever I've flown in from somewhere, I always try and go for a run. You feel so much better after, almost rejuvenated.'

There is a hint of an Australian twang to her voice these days. But she remains very much the idol of Ireland at large and her native Co. Cork in particular. As we talk, a series of men of varying vintage approach to commend her various achievements. The first rather gingerly says his piece, about-turns and flees. Another stays a while longer and starts reeling off names of people from Cobh whom she might know. Sonia nods and smiles in her own bashful manner and he departs feeling much the better for his encounter.

Sonia was born in Cobh on 28 November 1969, 33 days before the Swinging Sixties came to an end. Her grandfather Paddy O'Sullivan was a Dubliner who worked as a driver, delivering bottles of the black stuff all over Ireland for the Guinness Brewery. During his early years at the brewery, he met Josie Callanan, a young lady from the musical village of Doonbeg, Co. Clare. She was working in the dining hall at the Rupert Guinness Hall in Watling Street, where the annual Christmas concerts and variety shows were held.

When Paddy retired in 1975, the couple took on the lease of the Barge Inn in Robertstown, Co. Kildare. Sonia frequently visited the pub during her childhood, recalling it as a lively venue stuffed with people playing accordions and bodhráns. In 1998, when Mick O'Dwyer's Kildare footballers reached the All-Ireland final, she was amused to see that Robertstown had adopted her as one of their own pure-bred winners as part of their 'Up Kildare' campaign.

Sonia's father, John O'Sullivan, joined the Irish Navy and was stationed at the island harbour of Cobh. 'He would go away for a week or maybe two weeks at a time,' recalls Sonia. 'Killybegs was a name we used to hear a lot.' When the big naval vessels were docked in Haulbowline, John would take Sonia, her younger sister Gillian and younger brother Terry on board for an exploratory adventure. 'The Christmas party was always a big event.' That said, while she is a keen swimmer, she confesses that she did not inherit her father's sea legs and prefers to lub it on the land.

Sonia's mother was born Mary Shealy and grew up in Cobh. Her father, Michael, was the youngest of nine children born to Jimmy Shealy, a farmer from Kilbehenny, a quiet rural community in the Galtee Mountains, close to Mitchelstown. During the last decade of the nineteenth century, Jimmy was amongst the more prominent players on the Galtee Gaels football team.

Michael's mother passed away when he was a baby and the Shealy family appear to have scattered in later life, with many of the daughters becoming nuns and settling in America. Sonia recalls visiting cousins in Kilbehenny in her childhood. 'My grandparents sometimes took me to visit the relations, which was great because that meant I'd get some orange and other treats on the journey.' At the Shealys' farmhouse, she was mesmerised by an ancient wheel their great-aunt would turn to fan the kitchen fire.

Michael Shealy found work in the dockyard at Cobh, which is where he was living when his daughter Mary struck up with a naval officer called John O'Sullivan.

Sonia was the eldest of their three children. She was not particularly quick to start walking as a toddler. Nor did she commence running properly until she was at her secondary school, Cobh Vocational. Like many an athlete, she developed her passion by running to and from school.

'I tried to join in with the camogie because I felt that, being fit from running, I could assist the team and have fun doing it. But I wasn't very coordinated with stop-start running, or picking up the sliotar on the hurley. I just wasn't very good at team sports. I found it difficult being constrained by rules and other players. I felt so much freer running. I was also a bit scared that I'd get injured and be unable to run. And then I worked out that I was winning races, and that I could probably win a few more if I actually trained a little.'

Together with some friends, she joined the Ballymore-Cobh Athletics Club and began to train. And she hasn't stopped since. 'I don't like to go a day without running,' she says. 'If you keep doing it every day, you enjoy it a lot more. You go to bed knowing you're going to run the next day and you have it in your mind where you are going to run.'

Her success earned her a scholarship to Pennsylvania's Villanova University, where she studied accountancy. In 1990, the 21 year old became the National Collegiate Athletic Association's 3,000 m champion. She then ran the 3,000 m at the European Championships in Split and finished 11th. Her track record improved radically thereafter, and the following year she set her first world indoor record, winning the 5,000 m in Boston. At the World Student Games in Sheffield that summer she scored a gold in the 1,500 m and silver in the 3,000 m.

And so her extraordinary story moved into a new phase, as she scaled the ranks to become the greatest female athlete in Irish history. At one point she set five new national records in the space of eleven days.

'When I was growing up, I didn't know you could do sport as a job,' she says. 'It wasn't about money. I used to run races where the prize was a tracksuit or a pair of runners.'

At the Barcelona Olympics in 1992, she hit the lead in the final lap of the 3,000 m but was ultimately outsprinted to finish fourth. An 11th place in the 1,500 m semi-final also disappointed but she made amends by winning the 5,000 m in the 1992 Grand Prix final. At the 1993 World Championships in Stuttgart, she won silver in the 1,500 m.

The years 1994 and 1995 were golden ones and Sonia emerged as a true world champion, running the 1,500 m, 1 mile, 2,000 m and 3,000 m faster than any other female athletes during both of those years. An upset stomach kiboshed her Olympic dreams at Atlanta in 1996 and she went adrift for a while before bouncing back at the 1998 World Cross-Country Championships in Marrakesh to win two cross-country golds over the 4 km and 8 km courses. At the European Athletics Championships, she blew the opposition away with her gold-winning debut in the 10,000 m.

At the 2000 Olympics in Sydney, Sonia won a well-deserved silver in the 5,000 m. That was arguably the zenith of her running career. Few could doubt that she was extremely unlucky not to come away with a gold after her participation in four separate Olympic Games, not least when taken ill on the eve of the 5,000 m final at Athens in 2004.

'We all want to do our best,' she says. 'If you're having people around for dinner, you want it to be really good. But there are always going to be a lot of little steps to take along the way. And sometimes it doesn't go as you planned. You can't look too far ahead. You can't put the cart before the horse.'

These days, Sonia reckons she runs up to 70 miles every week. 'I went for a short run the other day and it was 50 minutes long so I was questioned afterwards on my definition of a short run!' She continues to compete frequently. In 2008, Sonia managed the Australian team for the 2008 IAAF World Cross-Country Championships in Edinburgh, and was deputy chef de mission of the highly successful European Youth Olympic squad in 2009.

She returns to Ireland for long stints five or six times a year and is otherwise based between Melbourne and London. She adores the dull moments on the rare occasions that they come along, when she gets to kick back with a newspaper or play with her two daughters.

Sonia will be chef de mission for Team Ireland's 2012 London Olympics campaign.

Sonia O'Sullivan powers onwards to achieve another personal best and set a new national record of 30:53.37 in the women's 10,000 m final at the Sydney Olympics in 2000. During the same games, she won the silver in the 5,000 m to become only the second Irish woman to bring home an Olympic medal. (© Brendan Moran/Sportsfile)

DAME MARY PETERS

Athletics

ACHIEVEMENTS

Olympics
1964, pentathlon, 4th
1968, pentathlon, 9th
1972, pentathlon, gold

Commonwealth Games
1966, shot-put, silver
1970, pentathlon, gold; shot-put, gold
1974, pentathlon, gold

AWARDS
BBC Sports Personality of the Year, 1972
Texaco Sportstar Award, 1970, 1972
MBE, 1973
CBE, 1990
Texaco Sportstars Hall of Fame, 1997
Dame Commander of the British Empire, 2000
Lifetime Achievement Award, *Sunday Times* Sportswoman of the Year Awards, 2001
Lord Lieutenant of the County Borough of Belfast, 2010

Two tons of sand is possibly not every girl's ideal 16th birthday present. Nor for that matter is a shot-put circle, complete with stop block. But when Arthur Peters presented them to his only daughter, Mary, he could be confident that such gifts would be greatly appreciated. And many years later, he would be rewarded for his foresight when he embraced Mary amid the bright lights of Munich shortly after she had won a gold medal at the 1972 Olympics.

Robert Henry Peters, Mary's grandfather, was a builder and stonemason who lived in the once affluent village of Woolton near Liverpool. His wife Mary grew up on a farm near Sedbergh in Yorkshire. Family lore recalls how Mary single-handedly escorted a cow by train all the way from Sedbergh to her brothers' dairy in Woolton. She evidently impressed Mr Peters and the couple were married in Woolton's Methodist chapel in the spring of 1900.

Seven children followed, of whom Mary's father Arthur was the third. In his youth, he developed a tremendous passion for working with animals, initially breeding rabbits and mice for Liverpool's laboratories, and later working in a fish and poultry shop. During the

1930s, he became an insurance agent with the Liverpool Victoria Friendly Society (LV), rising to become manager.

In his spare time, Arthur was leading violinist with the Liverpool Philharmonic Orchestra and, prior to his marriage, he reputedly practised for eight hours a day. His daughter dutifully had a stab at playing the violin herself. 'I never found it comfortable holding it under my chin,' says Mary. 'So I ended up holding a shot-put under there instead.'

Mary's mother, Hilda Ellison, was raised in the small agricultural village of Speke, near the present day John Lennon Airport in Liverpool. While England reeled from the effects of the economic recession in the 1930s, Hilda helped her mother run the family home while her father and three brothers threshed on surrounding farms.

In 1935, she met and married Arthur Peters and the couple settled in the Liverpudlian suburb of Halewood, where their son John was born in 1936. Mary was born on 6 July 1939.

Although they were not particularly sporty themselves, Arthur and Hilda encouraged their children to spend as much time outdoors as possible. 'Our childhood was basically set against the backdrop of the Second World War,' says Mary. 'My parents told us to get outside as much as we could, so that we could benefit from the vitamins of the sunshine and enjoy ourselves playing in the fields.' Naturally she began to compete with her brother, running, sprinting and even wrestling. 'That's what made me strong,' she says.

In the late 1940s, Arthur was assigned to serve as a part-time inspector at the LV office in Belfast. For the next two years, his children only saw him every second weekend. However, things changed in 1950 when Arthur became manager of the LV's district office in Ballymena. Hilda, 14-year-old John and 11-year-old Mary soon made the journey across the sea to their new homeland in Co. Antrim.

At school in Ballymena, Mary developed an extraordinary passion for athletics. Later on, at Portadown College, her Olympic destiny quickly manifested itself as she became house captain, captain of hockey and athletics and then head girl. Deeply inspired by her remarkable prowess, Mary's headmaster Donald Woodman introduced her to a past pupil called Kenneth McClelland, who was by then a PE trainer of renown. It was at about this time that her father poured two tons of sand into a field at the back of the house, whereon she could practise her long jump and high jump.

But Arthur knew his daughter's talents stretched considerably wider than mere jumping. 'My strongest event at that time was the shot-put,' says Mary. And so, alongside the sands came the shot-put circle. 'I started to break the Northern Irish record but it turned out the shots I was using were not the correct weight, so the record didn't count. My father went to the foundry to get an accurate shot made and I soon broke the record properly. It held for something like 42 years.'

By now it was clear that Mary's forte was the pentathlon, comprising the 80 m hurdles, shot-put, high jump, long jump and a 200 m sprint. The pentathlon was invented by Jason, he of the Argonauts and Golden Fleece fame. Jason's friend Peleus, father of Achilles, was the first man to win the event. And amongst those who enjoyed watching the sport was Aristotle, who remarked that pentathletes required 'a body capable of enduring all efforts, either of the racecourse or of bodily strength . . . This is why the athletes in the pentathlon are most beautiful.'

By the time Mary was 16, Mr McClelland had trained her sufficiently for her to compete in her first pentathlon at the 1956 Northern Irish Championships. The event was won by Thelma Hopkins, who broke the world high jump record that same year. Silver went to Irish Olympian Maeve Kyle. And the bronze went to a 16-year-old schoolgirl from Portadown called Mary Peters. Later that year, she went one better at the British Championships in Birmingham and came home with a silver.

Mary started work as a domestic science teacher, graduating from Belfast Tech to teach at Graymount Girls' Secondary School. Meanwhile, in 1958, she was on the Northern Irish team that went to the Commonwealth Games in Cardiff. She remained on the team for every Commonwealth Games until 1974, winning two gold medals for the pentathlon, as well as gold and silver for the shot-put.

Her coach Buster McShane was convinced that Olympic glory awaited. Under his careful supervision, Mary went to both the 1964 and 1968 Olympics, coming fourth and ninth respectively in the pentathlon. During the latter contest, she was team captain and she believes her performance suffered simply because she took her responsibilities too seriously.

As she edged into her fourth decade in 1970, one might have expected Mary to bow out gracefully. Not a bit of it.

'Oh, yes, there was a steel there,' she says. 'There has to be! It is not easy winning a gold medal and it is the one that matters.'

Northern Ireland's Mary Peters hurls herself along the sands during the long jump event of the pentathlon at the 1972 Munich Olympics. She duly returned to Belfast with an Olympic gold. (© Douglas Miller/Keystone/Getty Images)

Mary competed in the pentathlon again at the 1972 Olympics in Munich, giving the most jaw-dropping performance of her career. When the final points were calculated, Mary and Buster were informed that not only had she amassed a world record 4,801 points, with personal bests in all five events, but she had also won an Olympic gold medal. Her score still stands as the world record to this day.

Belfast erupted with delight as the victorious duo returned from Munich, an event overshadowed by Buster's tragic death in a car crash six months later.

On the night that she won her gold medal, a journalist from the *Belfast Telegraph* asked Mary how she would like to be commemorated. She replied that she would like to see a purpose-built racetrack opened up in Belfast. In 1974, shortly after the Mary Peters Track opened, the six-lane track was given a massive publicity boost when Mary, aged thirty-five, won a third gold at the Commonwealth Games in Christchurch, New Zealand.

Mary maintained a strong link to Britain's Olympic team, managing the women athletes from 1979 to 1984, during which time they won one gold, two silver and fifteen bronze medals at the 1980 and 1984 Olympics.

Since her retirement, she has continued to be a powerhouse for the promotion of both sport and community development across Ulster, as well as patron of innumerable charities. Not surprisingly the honours have come thick and fast. An MBE in 1973, a CBE in 1990 and, in 2000, she was appointed Dame Commander of the British Empire. She also established the Ulster Sports Trust, now relaunched as the Mary Peters Trust, which seeks to develop sporting prowess across the province. In January 2010, Dame Mary Peters took office as Lord Lieutenant of the County Borough of Belfast. She's come a long way since Liverpool.

JOHN TREACY

Athletics

ACHIEVEMENTS

Olympics
1984, marathon, silver

Marathons
Los Angeles, 1992, 1st
Dublin, 1993, 1st

World Cross-Country Championships
1978, long race, gold
1979, long race, gold; team long race, silver

AWARDS
Texaco Sportstars Award, 1978, 1979, 1984
Texaco Special Achievement Award, 1979

As he charged into the final stages of the 5,000 m at Crystal Palace in 1980, Olympic gold medallist Steve Ovett began to salute the applauding crowd. He looked to his left and saw a small Irishman cantering alongside him. Mr Ovett threw him a dismissive glance, accelerated and continued to wave at the crowd. However, just as he raised his arms to break through the ribbon, the Englishman saw the Irishman slip under him to get there first. The crowd exhaled, Mr Ovett expleted and John Treacy of Villierstown, Co. Waterford, secured perhaps not his most famous win but certainly one of his most audacious.

The Treacy family has been based in Villierstown for many generations. According to the 1911 census, John's grandfather Redmond 'Tracy' was born in 1877 and worked as a baker. By the time John's late father, Jack, was born in 1916, Redmond had added a general store to the bakery. In his youth, Jack drove a horse and cart around the surrounding parish, delivering bread every morning.

Jack managed to stave off marriage until he was 37 years old. 'He had a good bachelor-hood, you know that sort of a way,' laughs John. He kept fit playing both Gaelic football and rugby at local level but, says John, 'His real passion was the greyhounds, both racing and coursing . . . from the time that I was a young lad, I remember my dad walking the dogs. He bred them and he sold them and he'd be looking for new ones all the time. He'd deal on the phone and seal it with a handshake. They call them "doggy men".'

Jack's wife Gertie O'Brien came from the neighbouring village of Aglish, where her family had a convenience shop and post office. They had four children, Patrica, Ray and the twins, John and Liz, who were born in 1957. In 1963, Jack and Gertie closed down the bakery and opened up as a post office cum telephone exchange.

John began to run seriously during his first year at secondary school in Cappoquin. His brother Ray was by then running cross-country for his club in Waterford's An Rinn Galteacht region. Ray invited John to come along. 'We trained on a cattle farm near our house,' recalls John. 'It was better to be running on grass than on the road. Liz ran with us as well.'

Gladdened by the Treacys' enthusiasm, Fr Michael Enright, the club manager, put them in touch with legendary Strawberry Hill physiologist Tom Reilly. 'Tom started writing training schedules and posting them to us.' The schedules were instrumental in helping the youngsters develop into athletes of international renown.

In Waterford, the Treacys were joined by two others, Tony Ryan and Gerry Deegan. 'We all pushed each other along. One of us would win one day and another the next. It raised the bar and we all became internationals.'

One day, during his last year at school, John passed his bag to Liz and set off to run home from Cappoquin. The journey was normally five miles, but John went the long way around, racking up nine miles a day. 'That's how I really got started,' he says. 'I wanted to see what I could get out of myself.'

Before long, he was winning junior and Under-18 Munster and All-Ireland titles in cross-country, as well as the 1,500 m and 3,000 m. His success resulted in his selection for the Irish squad that competed at the 1974 World Junior Cross-Country Championships, in which he won bronze. 'It was a huge surprise to everyone, including myself, but it confirmed in my mind that running was what I should do.'

When he got home to Villierstown, the phone began ringing. 'American coaches, trying to get me go to their university. Jumbo Elliott from Villanova even visited me at home. That was probably one of the few recruitment trips he ever made!'

But Bob Amato from Providence College, Rhode Island, was the coach who 'did the best selling job'. John spent the next four years with the Dominicans at Providence and 'loved every minute of it'. 'To go from Villierstown to Rhode Island in 1974 was such a big culture change.' He studied business and focused on his running. 'There was twenty of us on the cross-country team. We came from all over the world but we all had the same passion. We all wanted to be world-beaters.'

John trained hard and, during his fourth year, he took 'a gigantic step forward' by finishing second to Henry Rono in the NCAA cross-country championships. In March 1978, he won the NCAA indoor three-mile championship.

'And two weeks later I ran over hill and dale to win the World Cross-Country Championships in Glasgow. It was very windy, wet and freezing cold and I was covered in mud. Three of us got away in the last thousand metres, then I ran away from the other two and held it to the end. That was a good day.'

John left Providence in 1978. The following year he won his second world cross-country title in Limerick, urged on by a crowd of 30,000 home supporters. 'It was wind and rain and cold again. But if you grew up running in Villierstown, you're used to that.

'I wouldn't be the most stylish runner in the world,' he says. 'But I know what it takes.

You can always say, "I am the best in the world," All the positive thinking in the world ain't going to help you if you haven't got the work done. But if you do train and get to the right level, then you will have the confidence – and the psychology almost takes care of itself.'

John's next big moment was the Moscow Olympics, for which he was 'in the shape of my life'. However, just 200 m from the finish line of his heat in the 10,000 m final, he was overwhelmed by dehydration and collapsed unconscious on the trackside. He somehow recovered to qualify for the final, where he came a creditable seventh. His surprise victory over Steve Ovett at Crystal Palace came just a couple of weeks later.

Returning to Ireland, John went to work full time with the Export Board. He married Fionnuala and became a father. But, most critically, he suffered two injuries, a fracture in his back and a knee injury, which curtailed his training.

Injury did not stop his desire to run. In 1983, the Treacys decided to return to America, to the competitive environment where John had excelled. They made their way to Providence, where John reunited with his former colleagues and began running. It took several months to get back in action. And then, at a road race in Connecticut on Thanksgiving Day in 1983, he raced Eamonn Coghlan all the way to the finish line. 'As he crossed the line, Eamonn turned to me and said, "You're back."'

John thanked Eamonn in the summer of 1984 by breaking the Dubliner's 5,000 m Irish national record. At the Los Angeles Olympics, John competed in the 10,000 m but

In March 1979, huge crowds gathered along the muddy sidelines of the old Limerick Racecourse to watch John Treacy cross the line to win the World Cross-Country Championships.
(© Ray McManus/Sportsfile)

disappointed. Five days later, he set off for the marathon at the Santa Monica Track Club. 'It was my first marathon, my maiden journey.' He came home with an Olympic silver, finishing 35 seconds after the winner Carlos Lopes. Their respective finishes remain the two fastest marathon times in Olympic history.

The Treacys continued to live in Providence until 1994, during which time John was a professional athlete sponsored by New Balance running shoes. In 1992, he won the Los Angeles Marathon and the following year he won the Dublin Marathon. However, when he realised that he no longer really minded if he won or not, he decided to call it quits. The Treacys now live in the hills by Saggart, while John is kept busy as the chief executive of the Irish Sports Council and a board member of Concern. He keeps fit by running and playing golf.

DENNY HYLAND

Athletics and Gaelic Football

Pole Vault
All-Ireland Championships: 10
Record height: 12 ft 5 in., 1957

Gaelic Football
Clubs: O'Hanrahans, Eire Og, Shamrocks

'I started out with a curtain pole when I was nine years of age. I was friendly with James Dempsey, whose family had a hardware shop in Carlow. They had the poles. And I got fond of the vaulting.'

Denny's octogenarian eyes remain steady as those gathered in the room whoosh at the thought of a nine year old whizzing through the skies at one end of a curtain pole. But such are the diminutive beginnings of mighty champions.

Fast-forward twenty years and the same small boy was midway through an epic reign which saw him win the annual All-Ireland Pole-Vaulting Championships on ten occasions, including a straight run of nine from 1952 to 1960.

Sport is in the blood. The Hylands were originally tenant farmers of the Earls of Portarlington and lived north-east of Portlaoise in a landscape called The Heath. Denny's grandfather and father, both called Michael, were born on the farm in 1852 and 1886 respectively. Michael junior was all set to inherit the farm and had developed a passion for the active life. 'He played Gaelic football and cricket,' says Denny. 'Lord Portarlington would bring teams to play at Emo Court and all the tenant farmers would make an opposing team.'

However, shortly before the First World War, the Hylands ran into a crisis when their two main corn-cutting machines broke down. Michael senior was obliged to sell the farm and relocated to Emo. His seven sons moved to Carlow Town, where Michael junior and another brother ran a pub on Tullow Street. Like many a publican before and since, they found their generosity got the better of them and they made no money. 'They just weren't able to run it,' says Denny with a sympathetic shake of the head. And so they sold the pub and Michael junior became a fitter, working first at Richard's Foundry in Carlow, and later as a lorry driver and labourer at The Shamrock. Denny would similarly spend most

of his working life with Thompson Engineering at Carlow's Hanover Works, and later at the town's Hydro Hoist factory.

Michael junior continued to play sport when he moved to Carlow, playing cricket at the club in Palatine and, in the absence of a senior team, playing county football for the Carlow juniors. In 1913, he played for the junior team that went on to win the Leinster Championship.

Denny's mother, Molly, was born in Dublin but came of Carlow stock. Her father Mathew Whelan hailed from a farm at Tomard near Milford and ran a pub in Leighlinbridge. 'Aye, there was a lot of pubs in the family at one point,' says Denny, 'farms and pubs.'

Michael and Molly married in 1923 and had four boys and three girls. 'I was third from the bottom or fourth from the top,' offers Denny, who arrived in May 1929. He was brought up on Tullow Street, just opposite the Presentation Convent, and educated by the Christian Brothers.

Not surprisingly, the Hyland children all inherited an instinctive zeal for sport. Denny's three sisters were feisty table-tennis players. His eldest brother, Michael, was frequently to be seen swimming in Carlow's rivers and, adds Denny's wife Delma, he was 'fairly handy with a hula hoop too'. His late brother Paddy played both rugby and Gaelic football; he was on the team with Denny when O'Hanrahans won the Carlow county final in 1945. As for the younger brother, Brendan, 'I'm not sure if you'd call it sport, but he was good at playing cards.'

Sporting options were something of a rarity in Denny's childhood. 'It was during the war years and they hadn't the price of a football,' he explains. 'There were some league matches but there were no matches between schools in my time.' On Wednesday afternoons the kids would make their way to run around a sports field on Carlow's Green Road, where the regiments of the British Empire had drilled half a century earlier.

Denny was the sportiest of the Hyland siblings. From O'Hanrahans, he became one of the star players with the Shamrocks (Carlow's town team), winning the 1949 Carlow junior football clubs final. He also donned the red, green and yellow jersey of his county to play half-back for their National Football League campaigns throughout the early 1950s. He won the Dr Humphrey's Cup at the Carlow Championships for the best all-round athlete in 1952, 1953 and 1954.

But it was as a pole-vaulter that he became a household name across Ireland. It seems likely people have been using sticks and poles to shoot into the skies since the invention of hands, particularly in marshy areas. The first definitive pole vault competitions appear to be those held in Ireland during the Tailteann Games, which took place in the second millennium BC. It had re-emerged as a competitive sport in Cumbria by the 1840s and was one of the most popular events at the inaugural modern Olympics in 1896.

At school, Denny was often to be seen vaulting walls and hedges with a rough-cut pole. 'We were doing 6 ft and thought we were great,' he laughs. At the age of 18, he became more serious about it, using a 10-ft bamboo pole to clear a timber lath, taking exact measurements every time he landed. 'Timing is everything,' he counsels, 'and relaxation.' Sometimes he landed hard. 'I never jumped on a mattress in my life,' he says. And yet he never gave himself an injury.

In 1948, the 19 year old competed for the first time at the All-Ireland Youth Championships, and won bronze with a jump of 9 ft 5 in. The following year, he won the contest and broke the Irish record for the first time with a vault of 11 ft 5 in. in Enniscorthy. Just minutes later his friend and rival Val McGann of Ballinasloe, Co. Galway, cleared 11 ft 7 in. in the same contest. But in July 1951, Denny set a new record at the annual Guinness Sports at Iveagh Grounds, Crumlin, with 11 ft 8 ¾ in., and this time it held.

Throughout the 1950s, Denny dominated at the three main annual contests – the All-Ireland Championships, the Leinster Championships and the Cork City Sports Championships. Every year the good-looking vaulter from Carlow vaulted a little higher – and the crowds who came to watch got a little bigger. The *Irish Times* declared that he had 'stolen the limelight' at the 1955 NACA (National Athletic and Cycling Association) All-Ireland Championships when he soared over the lath to become the first Irishman to vault 12 ft, reaching 12 ft 2 in. He ultimately jumped 12 ft 5 in., which was more than a foot higher than the record when he started.

'The *Sunday Press* were always publishing his picture,' recalls Delma proudly. Delma Fenelon was a fun-loving bootmaker's daughter who lived around the corner from Denny on Barrack Street. 'We were neighbours and he was friends of my brother,' she says. 'He used to go with other girls in between. A lot of girls. But as someone says to me, "You got him in the end, Delma!"' And did she have any vaulting ambitions herself? 'I did not!'

They were married on St Valentine's weekend of February 1960; five children followed. Their son Michael, trained by Denny, later won the Irish championships with a jump of 14 ft 6 in. Sport remains in the blood, with a granddaughter who hurdles and a grandson who is a promising tennis player.

JUNE ANN FITZPATRICK

Tennis

ACHIEVEMENTS
Roland Garros French Open, semi-finals (doubles), 1958
Wimbledon, quarter-finals (mixed and ladies' doubles), 1957
Irish Senior Ladies' Championships, winner, 1950, 1951
Irish Under-18s Ladies' Championships, winner, 1949, 1950
Irish Under-15s Ladies' Championships, 1946, 1947
Festival of Britain Championship, winner, 1951
Championships of Northern California, winner, 1955
British Columbia Championship, winner, 1955
Championships of Oregon and Washington, winner, 1955

'And so I thought, now I can either burst into tears and run off the court, or I can get my little act together.' At the age of 21, the girl from Co. Cork had just received the first avalanche of knock-up balls across the net from the reigning New York champion. 'They came so fast I didn't see them, but I got my little act together and I won 6–4, 6–2 . . . and why not?' It was the autumn of 1954 and Ireland's indomitable ladies' champion had just begun her American conquest with a famous televised victory at Fordham University.

June Ann blames her older brother Gerry for starting her tennis career. On her 13th birthday, her father gifted her a tennis racket. 'Gerry remarked that I wouldn't be able to hit the house with a ball if I was beside it,' she says, eyes narrowing. 'I've never had an argument but I will fight all the way. That was the challenge and I decided I was going to play tennis.'

June Ann's father was John Fitzpatrick, the Cork-born engineer who, amongst many achievements, installed central heating in Leinster House, won the coveted Whitworth Award, founded the Welding Society of Ireland and orchestrated the rural drainage programme in the Midlands and West.

The Fitzpatricks lived in the village of Rushbrooke on the Great Island in Cork Harbour, where John was engaged in rebuilding the naval pier at Cobh and working with the Irish Naval Service. The pinewoods around her home would later inspire June Ann to call her Dublin house 'Torytops' after the pine cones, or torytops, which she collected as a child.

The Rushbrooke Lawn Tennis and Croquet Club is the oldest tennis club in Ireland

and it was here that June Ann first mastered the sport. She started out as something of a tomboy, albeit a well-dressed one. 'There were no other girls playing,' she says. 'I loved the tennis outfits and I made my own dresses. My skirts were very short but I had little trousers underneath to keep me decent.

'I liked the whole idea of sport because it lifted people's spirits. These were the Dark Ages. The war had devastated Europe and it was all very depressed.'

At 5 ft 8 ½ in., she was undoubtedly a daunting opponent, not least up at the net. She was also equally good on the left or right, forehand or backhand, enabling her to outfox the opposition in doubles matches by swapping positions.

In the summer of 1947, she entered the Munster Under-15s championship and won. 'And why not?' She then made her way to Dublin, where she won the Leinster and Ulster championships as well as the Fitzwilliam Cup to become Ireland's Under-15 champion. She won the same quartet the following year. Her success compelled Dublin's Lord Mayor Alfie Byrne to invite her to teach tennis to the children of the city's post-war slums on Mountjoy Square and Pearse Street.

In 1948, Tennis Ireland secured her a week's training, from seven to quarter past eight every morning. Her coach Hank Quinn was the man who trained the US Davis Cup team to victory that same year. 'If you have too many lessons, it can kill your natural instinct,' warns June Ann, 'but I was a very lucky little girl to have lessons from him.'

They met on the grass courts of the old Fitzwilliam Club on Lad Lane. 'He told me tennis is 90 per cent footwork and if you don't get that right, you may as well stay in bed.' He also taught her how to serve. 'Throw up the ball, move your hips, put your whole weight into it, keep your eye on the ball and don't drop your head.'

At lunchtime, she cycled back to the club from her school at the Sacred Heart on Leeson Street to serve over and over again, 'maybe a thousand times until I got it right'. It helped that the US team had a ready supply of the very latest tennis equipment. 'In Ireland, tennis balls were like gold dust at this time . . . and to wear a pair of rubber shoes, that was amazing!'

In 1948 and 1949, June Ann won the Irish junior championships. Shortly after she completed her Leaving Certificate, she went to Junior Wimbledon, where she was beaten by the eventual tournament champion, Lorna Cornell, 16–14 in the final set. Gerry also competed that year and the Fitzpatricks were thus the first brother and sister to play at Wimbledon together.

She went on to win back-to-back titles in the Irish senior ladies' championships before crossing the Irish Sea in May 1951 to win the prestigious Festival of Britain tennis tournament. 'They presented me with an enormous cup but I couldn't take it home because you weren't allowed to take any silver out of Britain in those days. So I took it to an uncle of mine who was a jeweller in London and he put my name on it in huge writing just to make sure everyone knew it was mine.'

In November 1954, the twenty-one-year-old Irish champion crossed the Atlantic on the ocean liner SS *America* to begin a three-year sojourn in the USA. She was ostensibly there to look after 35 post-war baby boomers at the Sacred Heart primary school in San Francisco. Her green card application was undoubtedly helped by the fact that one of her regular opponents at the Fitzwilliam was William Howard Taft, US Ambassador to Ireland and grandson of former US President Taft.

Before her teaching job began, she was briefly adopted by Gussie Moran, the Irish-American tennis star who had electrified Wimbledon in 1949 by sporting an extremely short tennis dress with ruffled, lace-trimmed knickers peeping out below the hem. 'Gorgeous Gussie' became an inspiration to June Ann and helped get her a short-term job in Macy's, selling German and Belgian handbags.

Early the next year, June Ann arrived in San Francisco. The convent had its own tennis courts where she could practise. Having already defeated the New York champion, June Ann entered the Northern California championships reasoning that 'even if this was America, there was only going to be one person the other side of the net so why shouldn't I be able to beat them?' She duly knocked out a Wightman Cup champion and defeated the Japanese No. 1 to win the trophy which now hangs proudly on her wall. 'That was a very prestigious tournament so it meant I could now travel around the USA, all expenses paid!'

She travelled for the three-month school holidays, winning several more trophies including the British Columbia championship for which she was ranked as the No. 1 seed. 'The evening before it I got an invitation to tea with the Governor General, which was quite something for a little Catholic girl from Co. Cork. They were so nice that I had to win it.' She also won several doubles contests; her American partner 'was a good player but I'd have walloped her in a sink!'

June Anne Fitzpatrick strikes back during the Irish Open tennis championships at the old Fitzwilliam Club on Dublin's Lad Lane in 1954. (Photographer unknown)

June Ann remained in the US for just under three years and qualified as an occupational therapist. Back in Ireland, although working full time, she entered Wimbledon, reaching the final 16 in both the ladies' and mixed doubles. In 1958, she 'trotted off' to Paris for the Roland Garros, where she reached the semi-finals in the mixed but lost while leading in the final set when her partner stood on a ball and broke his ankle.

In 1959, she married engineer Bernard Le Cesne Byrne and settled on a windy country lane just outside Dundrum. 'It was all farmland around here then. Sheep were always wandering onto our lawn and Dundrum was still a village where people got their messages delivered.'

'I'm supposedly retired,' she says, 'but life is for living.' And live she does. She frequently walks in the French Pyrenees, 20 km a day if she can. She raised a small fortune for Irish Guide Dogs for the Blind walking the 2009 mini-marathon in Dublin. She regularly tinkles upon the piano to keep her fingers and brain agile. She takes a daily dose of oils – primrose, cod liver and flax – and dotes upon Scooter, her trusty Wicklow collie.

Tennis remains at the centre of her life. And perhaps June Ann's proudest achievement was the founding of the Irish Evergreens, a club dedicated to developing tournaments for tennis players aged 40 and over. The Evergreens compete in contests all over the world and were at one point ranked No. 5. June Ann has won individual senior titles in the Netherlands, Russia, France and the Baltic states, and in 2005 she went to the Australian championships, where she became the No. 2 over-70 player in the world. 'You've got to see the funny side of it. If I'm playing in my age group, I can't do much damage.'

ROSEMARY SMITH

Rally Driving

MAJOR WINS
Tulip Rally, 1965
British Saloon Car Championship: 3
Coupes des Dames: 12
Outright Wins in Ireland: 3
Internationals: 24 (finished in 21, won 1, collected 12, 9 class wins, placed in her class 6 times)

AWARDS
Texaco Sportstars Award, 1965
Motorsport Ireland Hall of Fame, 2001

'Thinking back, it was all very dangerous. Two girls, out in the middle of nowhere, in Africa. The dead of night. I remember passing a hut with a noose hanging from a tree. That made me go a bit faster.'

Rosemary Smith is musing upon her triumphant outing for the 1973 East African Safari, when she and her navigator Pauline Gullack took their Datsun Bluebird 1800 on the 2,500-mile circuit of the Dark Continent to become the first ladies past the post.

Their journey began in Nairobi, from where they headed west through the Serengeti to the Victoria Falls, then east via Malawi to the coast at Mombasa and north again to Nairobi.

'There was no such thing as roads,' says Rosemary nonchalantly. 'Everything was gravel, dirt and dust until it rained and turned everything into thick red gumbo mud. But with those cars, if you stopped you just couldn't get going again, so we drove all day and right on through the night, for six days in a row, with an average speed of 83 miles an hour.'

Occasionally they passed rival cars, paused upon the roadside. The memory prompts a wicked chuckle from this veritable Penelope Pitstop. 'We drove right past them and knocked them further off the road if we could. I had a marker pen and I used to put a cross on the side of the car every time we knocked one, like bombers did in the war. I think our car ended up with something like 28 crosses down the side of it.'

Rosemary Smith was born in Dublin in 1937. Her father, the late John Metcalf Smith,

was a motor engineer of English pedigree who ran a garage in Rathmines. During her childhood, Rosemary frequently went to see her father, and later her elder brother, race Chryslers on circuits all over Ireland – Phoenix Park, Dunboyne, the Curragh and so forth. She became enamoured of the sport to such an extent that she was the leading female driver in the world in the 1960s.

At the age of 16, Rosemary left school and started a fashion business. One of her first clients was Delphine Biggar, a formidable lady whose husband Frank had won the 1956 Monte Carlo Rally.

When 'Mrs B' learned that 17-year-old Rosemary liked to drive, she invited her to navigate. Rosemary wasn't much of a navigator. On their first outing, their Mini fetched up straddling a gorse bush on top of a mountain with Mrs B cursing like a trooper. 'She might as well have said nothing to me because my dad was a very strict Methodist and I didn't understand swearing back then,' says Rosemary.

Mrs B decided that perhaps Rosemary would be better as a driver. It turned out to be a wise swap and, for the next 18 months, the duo won just about every rally they entered, speeding down every back road on the island, bounding over potholes and gliding around hairpins, usually at breakneck speed.

And then, one jet-black night, Mrs B directed Rosemary to go straight through the crossroads ahead. Rosemary duly whammed her foot on the accelerator. Three seconds later, crash. The crossroads was, in fact, a low stone country wall in Co. Kilkenny. The car flipped and rolled, blood splashed, Mrs B was out for the count and Rosemary had to move very, very fast if she was to prevent things becoming fatal. She squished out one of the Mini's sliding side windows, losing her shoes in the process. 'You always lose your shoes in an accident.' And then she ran through the dark night until she found a farmstead.

The farmer appeared, shotgun in hand. 'Bloody women drivers,' he muttered. They were unable to get Mrs B out of the Mini because the doors had buckled. So the farmer procured a sledgehammer and smashed a hole in the car, through which they dragged Mrs B. Four hours had passed by the time they finally reached the hospital in Carlow. Mrs B received 49 stitches to her head but she survived.

The following morning, Mrs B's husband put Rosemary behind the wheel of his car and ordered her to drive home. Had he not done that, there is every chance that Rosemary Smith would never have driven again.

But drive she did, and by 1960 Rosemary had established herself as one of the foremost drivers in Ireland. She started in a Triumph Herald, then switched to a Mini. In 1963, a bride-to-be asked Rosemary if they could do something exciting before she got married. 'She wanted to do Monte Carlo but she couldn't drive, so would I drive?' Along with a navigator, the girls headed to the south coast of France.

While in Monte Carlo, a senior member of the Rootes Group saw the Irish blonde and that was her breakthrough. She remained with Rootes for most of her racing career. In only her fifth year of rallying, and her first in a Hillman Imp, Rosemary won her greatest accolade, the 1965 Tulip Rally. Her victory in the Netherlands established her as the world's leading lady rally driver. The following year she won the Coupes des Dames in Monte Carlo but was controversially disqualified on the shaky grounds that her Lucas headlights were improper.

Marcus Chambers, her boss at Rootes, described her as 'the only lady rally driver I have

ever known who could arrive at the end of a very tough rally section and step out of the car looking neat and tidy and well dressed'. When the press asked what she carried in her purse, she replied, 'Lipstick, face powder, and the train schedule in case I break the car.'

The East Africa Safari was just one of several mind-bendingly long rallies Rosemary competed in. The London–Mexico Marathon, for instance, involves a gentle 5,000 miles around Europe followed by 12,000 miles around South America. 'It was all about endurance,' she says. 'But it's completely changed now. They only drive during the daytime and they have helicopters flying overhead to tell them there's a hole here and a boulder there. When we did East Africa, two hundred cars started and ten finished.'

During the 1968 London–Sydney, her carburettor burned a hole in one of the pistons of her MkII Lotus-Cortina while she was driving through Iran. With only three cylinders, the car was unable to climb the Khyber Pass in first gear. Full of initiative, Rosemary simply turned the Cortina around and reversed up the Khyber Pass.

In 1969, the French denied her entry into the 24 Heures du Mans on the grounds of her gender. At this time she left Rootes and moved to Ford in Ireland. In 1978, she broke the Irish land speed record in Cork as part of a bet with biker Danny Keany. She drove a Jaguar with an American V8 engine and clocked 178 mph. 'I went from 0–60 in a flash and I was driving over a ridged concrete road which kept jiggling my helmet over my eyes so I had one hand keeping that up and the other on the wheel.' However, a few moments later, her record was broken when Keany reached 204 mph on his 750-cc Yamaha motorcycle.

Shortly before she retired from racing in 2004, Rosemary had a bizarre and vivid dream

Rosemary Smith behind the wheel of a Fraser Imp for the 1966 Martini Trophy at Silverstone. (Photo courtesy of J.F. Steenhuis)

about a fatal crash involving a Jaguar on a hairpin bend of Belgium's Circuit de Spa-Francorchamps. She was due to compete in the race two weeks later but the dream scared her so much that she withdrew. On the day of the race, she rang a friend in Belgium to discover there had been a fatal crash involving a Jaguar on the very same hairpin bend. 'Now, when I dream of something, I really take heed of it.'

Rosemary is the honorary president of both the Imp clubs of England and Ireland and of Dunboyne Motorclub. She still travels a lot and gives demonstration drives, but she has no desire to compete any more. Since 1996, she has been teaching youngsters how to drive a normal car on a normal road. Based in Goffs in Co. Kildare, she has considerable empathy for teenagers endeavouring to learn on the busy roads of modern Ireland. She has also raised a large amount of money for Breast Cancer Research, most recently with the 2010 Rally Girls Uncut Calendar.

'I thought when I got to this ripe old age I'd be sitting at home doing my knitting,' she sighs. 'Absolutely no chance. But I would much prefer to be busy. I still drive the little Hillman Imp I drove in the rallies in the '60s. She's a little dote.'

NIALL O'TOOLE

Rowing

ACHIEVEMENTS

Men's Lightweight Coxless Fours
Olympics, 2004 (6th)
World Championships, 1996 (4th),
 1998 (4th)

Men's Lightweight Double Sculls
Olympics, 1996

RECORDS
World, men's lightweight single scull, 2 km, 1991

AWARDS
Texaco Sportstar Award, 1994

Men's Lightweight Single Sculls
Olympics, 1992 (20th)
World Championships, 1991 (gold), 1994
 (silver), 1995 (4th), 1996 (4th), 1998 (4th)
Under-23 World Championships, 1989
 (gold), 1990 (gold)

It is now 1,200 years since Turgesius the Norseman's longship sailed up the River Liffey in pursuit of a place to establish a trade outpost. The men who powered his longship must have had brawny shoulders, for Dublin is a long way from Norway. Presumably Turgesius scouted around the small island where the Liffey meets the River Camac. Certainly Vikings lived on this island; 18 of them were buried in a gravel ridge along its southern bank.

Today, the island is known as Islandbridge, the heart of Dublin's rowing quarter. Half a dozen rowing clubs amble along the Liffey's shores. Amongst these is the Commercial Rowing Club, established in 1856, which, as the name implies, drew its members from Dublin's commercial quarter – primarily bankers, tailors and shopkeepers.

The same waters that lapped against Turgesius' longboat now wash upon the Commercial's causeway. On the opposite shore, seagulls and guillemots swirl around a folly in Longmeadows Park. The air is still, the river bubbles, the trees are green. You could be in the middle of rural Ireland. But then a familiar whiff of hops drifts on a westerly breeze from the Guinness Brewery at St James's Gate. Niall O'Toole breathes it in with mixed emotions.

Niall was Ireland's first rowing world champion. His family have worked with Guinness for several generations. Seamus O'Toole, his grandfather, spent his life working as a shipwright, or ship's carpenter, for the brewery. 'He used to work on the boats that brought the Guinness over to Liverpool,' says Niall.

Jimmy O'Toole, Niall's father, served with the Merchant Navy in the Congo during the 1950s, before he too became a shipwright with Guinness. For many years, Jimmy was based at Birkenhead in Liverpool, where he was entrusted with fixing up Guinness ships like the *Lady Patricia* and *Lady Grania*. He later returned to Ireland and settled in Terenure, Co. Dublin, where, as well as working with Guinness and other nixers, Jimmy began building boats in his back yard.

'My father was a legend,' says Niall. 'He was the ultimate family man and way ahead of his time. When all the other fathers were down in the pub, he'd come home from work and take us down to the boat clubs, or onto the *Lady Patricia*, or out to the seaside. That was quite unique. No other fathers were doing that. He had a great affinity with boats and water and he involved us in everything.'

Niall left school at the age of seventeen and began a two-year carpentry apprenticeship. 'My dad maybe wasn't the most talented carpenter in the world,' he laughs, 'but he was a man of amazing patience and character. I was hanging off him 24-7, helping out, and I wanted to be a carpenter just like him.'

However, a new career option was simultaneously opening up to him. The O'Tooles are prodigious rowers. Niall's father rowed. So did his brother and so did his three sisters. In 1985, Niall began to row competitively for the Commercial and 'I realised I was reasonably good at it'. It started with his older brother. 'You always want to beat your brother, don't you?' he smiles. 'And then you want to beat the guy who beat your brother. There's a whole psychology of chasing the next victory.'

In 1989, the 19 year old decided to put his carpentry career on hold and turn professional as a single sculler. 'My mother was dead set against it but my father was full on, follow your dreams, son.

'I was probably the first Irishman to start training systematically and full time,' he says. 'I had a very good coach called Mick Desmond. He was a massive influence. But there was nothing really going on here in the rowing world in the late '80s and there was nobody I could measure myself against. That made it kind of a lonely gig.'

In order to find someone on the same level to train with, Niall went abroad. 'I spent a lot of time training in places like Italy and Belgium. That gave me access to their resources and I got to see how they trained and also how vulnerable they were. When you don't know someone, you can have all these magical, mystical beliefs about how brilliant they are. But when you live with them, you really get to know them and you see they're as fragile and fallible as you are, and that you could be as good as any of them.'

In 1991, Niall represented Ireland at the World Championships in Vienna and won the lightweight single scull to return home with the country's first gold medal in rowing. He simultaneously established a new world record, completing the 2,000 m distance in 6:49.17.

'I guess I was the first person in Irish rowing to make the breakthrough, but we've had a lot of success since then.' His victory kick-started a massive rowing revival in Ireland. 'We were lucky that our glory days coincided with the Celtic Tiger,' he says. 'We were getting the results

so the National Lottery were happy to pay for a new clubhouse here at the Commercial.' The Irish government also funded the National Rowing Centre at Inniscarra, Co. Cork.

From a personal perspective, the new influx of Irish rowing enthusiasts was a positive for the 6 ft 3 in. sculler. 'It was great to have people to train with. You live like a monk when you're rowing. I didn't want to be in a pub on a Friday night. I preferred to be rowing and training. So socialising went out the window. But there is great camaraderie and great crack between rowers. And there's absolutely nothing better than that collective feeling. You might give up certain stuff but you get your rewards. There's a trade-off.'

In 1999, Niall married physiotherapist Fiona O'Toole, who is now the Irish rowing team's physio. 'Rowing is one of the most physically demanding sports in the world. When we were training, we'd do about 35 hours a week. You need the power, but it's also about your endurance and muscles. I used to be an animal about it and I never thought about the risks or diets or things like that. But it was taking me a lot longer to recover. I had a few repetitive strain problems and my back was giving me pains from lifting too many weights. And all the guys I was up against were much younger than me. So I began to get more scientific about it all and I started picking my battles.'

With Fiona's encouragement, Niall went to the 2004 Olympics in Athens with the Irish team; they came home sixth. 'I was always better in the singles,' says Niall. 'Being on a team is very different. You can't be moody. You have to encourage your teammates and they will do the same for you.'

He did not take part in the 2008 Olympics but instead focused on establishing a post-rowing career. 'As in many sports, you tend to forsake your career for a long time. I didn't have my first job until I was 27 so I needed to get onto the ladder.' Having run his own business for a couple of years and worked with Golden Pages, Niall went to the Smurfit Business School. He is presently director of sponsorship for business and finance. Niall and Fiona have two children and live in Terenure.

At the Athens Olympics in 2004, Niall O'Toole (second from right) joined Paul Griffin, Eugene Coakley and Richard Archibald on Ireland's lightweight men's coxless fours team. Thirteen years earlier, the Dubliner won a gold medal for Ireland at the World Championships.
(© Brendan Moran/Sportsfile)

DAVE FINLAY JR

Wrestling

'Some people call me a fighting Irish bastard,' growled Dave Finlay Jr, 'but NOT TO MY FACE!' With this immortal catchphrase, the wrestler from Carrickfergus launched his brilliant comeback in 2006 as one of the star performers of the multimillion-dollar World Wrestling Entertainment (WWE) business.

To date, Dave has held 22 titles, including the British Heavyweight Championship, the WCW World Television Championship and the WWE United States Championship. He presently operates as a trainer in WWE and is a member of the SmackDown roster.

Wrestling as a sport appears to be as old as humanity itself. It was the pastime of choice for the ancient Greeks and featured prominently in the original Olympic Games. Henry VIII of England was an enthusiast. International freestyle wrestling was codified in 1920, and by the 1970s the sport was winning huge numbers of fans across the world.

Dave was raised on the shores of Belfast Lough during the 1960s and 1970s, and wrestling was part of his life from his earliest age. 'I was brought up in a family of wrestlers,' he says. 'Both my grandfathers were wrestlers and so was my dad. My sister was a referee and my mother helped my dad run the actual wrestling business.'

Dave's paternal grandfather, William John Finlay, was a Presbyterian blacksmith's son from Muckamore, Co. Antrim. Born in 1904, he was regularly to be found both wrestling and boxing in Ulster's fairground booths in his younger days. Dave's other grandfather,

John Douglas Liddell, was born in 1914 and became an active promoter of the sport in Belfast in the mid-twentieth century.

Born in Whiteabbey, Co. Antrim, in 1936, Dave's father David Finlay Sr was a master of both the Olympic freestyle and pro wrestling styles, performing at venues across Britain and Ireland. He went on to organise some of the very first freestyle wrestling bouts ever witnessed in Ireland. During the 1970s, he and his son travelled together all over the country, promoting wrestling in an age that coincided with the rise of the late great Martin 'Giant Haystacks' Ruane, whose parents were from Co. Mayo.

Dave began wrestling at the age of eight, perfecting the Olympic freestyle. From his early teens, his father also trained him in the pro style.

In 1974, deliberately or not, another wrestler no-showed for a bout Finlay Sr was promoting in the village of Glynn outside Larne. Fourteen-year-old Dave slipped into his father's boots and trunks, stepped into the ring and a star was born.

Over the next four years, with his father as trainer, Dave wrestled full time across Ireland, providing welcome entertainment in a time of political strife. He then moved to England, where he was spotted and signed up by British Wrestling Federation President Orig Williams.

In June 1982, the Ulsterman secured his first major title, becoming British heavy middleweight champion, before going on to defeat Ringo Rigby to win the British light heavyweight title.

During the early 1980s, Dave repeatedly won and lost the world mid-heavyweight title, frequently trading it with English wrestler Marty Jones, who became the first of his many nemeses. He also won the All Star British Heavyweight Championship, which enabled him to team up with Jones and win Germany's Catch Wrestling Association tag title.

He remained a major player on the European and Japanese circuits throughout the 1980s, regaining the British heavy middleweight title in 1987.

In the early 1980s, Dave enjoyed some TV stardom on ITV's *World of Sport*, most memorably when pitted against 'The American Dream', Steve Adonis. Sporting a greased mullet, Dave was managed by his then wife Princess Paula.

His on-screen appeal was further enhanced in 1996 when *Monday Nitro*, the weekly wrestling show, broadcast a parking lot brawl between Dave and Lord Steven Regal, one of the icons of an English wrestling stable called the Blue Bloods. Their notorious feud culminated in a showdown at the Tupelo Coliseum in Mississippi, during which, fighting as the Belfast Bruiser, Dave was attacked by the Blue Bloods and broke Regal's nose.

Dave's antics caught the attention of Ted Turner's World Championship Wrestling (WCW) in Atlanta, Georgia, who invited him to come on board. He re-emerged as 'Fit Finlay' and, with a little push, pinned Texan hulk Booker T to win the WCW World Television Championship in 1998.

As well as his trademark Rolling Fireman's Carry Slam move, Dave was now a specialist in back-breakers, brain-busters and, his preferred finish, the Tombstone Piledriver. In 1998, he also became a born-again Christian.

In July 1999, Dave won the Hardcore Junkyard Invitational in Florida. However, just days later, his career hung on a thread after he was thrown onto a glass table in Jackson, Mississippi, during a contest. The table shattered, badly lacerating a nerve in his leg. Although he regained the use of his leg, the momentum of his Junkyard victory was lost and he was 'out' of the game for nearly five years, during which time he began training young wrestlers for the WWE.

He returned to the ring in 2003, hamming it up as a proud Irishman. Perhaps his greatest fight took place in April 2006, when he delivered a Celtic Cross to defeat the late Canadian champion Chris Benoit in the 'King of the Ring' contest. Dave was pinned in the semi-finals by his great rival, martial artist Bobby Lashley. Their match coincided with another televised parking lot brawl in which Lashley attempted to overturn a car onto him. Dave went on to seize Lashley's United States Championship crown.

In ensuing contests, Dave's Oirishness was complemented by the frequent assistance of 'the Little Bastard', a 4 ft 4 in. midget from Wisconsin, also known as Hornswoggle, who came on stage dressed as a leprechaun. Wrestling lore subsequently held that the Little Bastard was Dave Finlay's son.

Nearly forty years after his first bout, Dave continues to impress as a wrestler, trading to the SmackDown brand in June 2009. 'I've been around a while and I know all the tricks,' says the ginger-haired veteran. 'I'm just as tough as I ever was. It's a great business to be in but you've got to look after yourself.'

He has three children by his German wife Manuela. David, his eldest son, was born in 1993 and has already followed in the family footsteps and taken to the ring. The Finlays live in Georgia but return to visit Ireland whenever opportunity knocks.

Dave also operates as a road agent, or producer, planning storylines and helping young wrestlers, particularly women, to set up matches. He is also working with Dublin-born WWE champion Sheamus. His father continues to teach youngsters at the Knockagh Raiders Wrestling Club in Greenisland, just outside Carrickfergus.

GER McKENNA

Greyhound Racing

NOTABLE WINS
English Derby, 1981, 1989
Waterloo Cup, 1984
English Laurels, 1990
Irish Derby, 1969, 1973, 1987
Irish Oaks, 1979
Irish St Leger, 1956, 1960, 1962, 1965, 1967,
   1969, 1971, 1972, 1976, 1977, 1984
Irish Laurels, 1970, 1976, 1980, 1983, 1984,
   1985, 1996

AWARDS
Texaco Sportstars Award, 1965, 1966, 1967,
   1973, 1981
Greyhound Racing Sportsman of the Year,
   1981, 1984, 1987
Greyhound Hall of Fame, 1998

'There's a lot of luck in it, to be straight with you,' concedes Ger McKenna. 'You could take a bitch to a dog and you might think it would breed the bee's knees. But the pups mightn't win a race between them. And then you might go to some ordinary auld dog and get a great litter out of it. Don't listen to the fellow who says this is the dog for him or this is the bitch for her. It's solid luck.'

Ger McKenna should know. The eighty year old from Borrisokane, Co. Tipperary, has built up one of the most remarkable trophy collections in the greyhound game, racking up forty-four classic wins, including two English Derbys and the coveted Waterloo Cup. 'Himself and Lester Piggott used to be neck and neck,' says his wife Josie proudly.

The McKennas have been breeding and training greyhounds since the nineteenth century. Ger's grandfather Michael McKenna was a toddler when the legendary Master McGrath scored his Waterloo Cup treble between 1868 and 1871. Michael later became a prosperous merchant-farmer and Ger remembers him walking greyhounds up the roads around their farm.

Michael and his wife had thirteen children and, says Ger, 'every one of them had an interest in dogs'. Ger's father Malachy was the third child, born in 1889, and often talked about the 'tough times before the first war'. Malachy farmed outside Borrisokane, secured his trainer's licence and kept about 30 dogs. He also had 13 children. 'They weren't sleeping

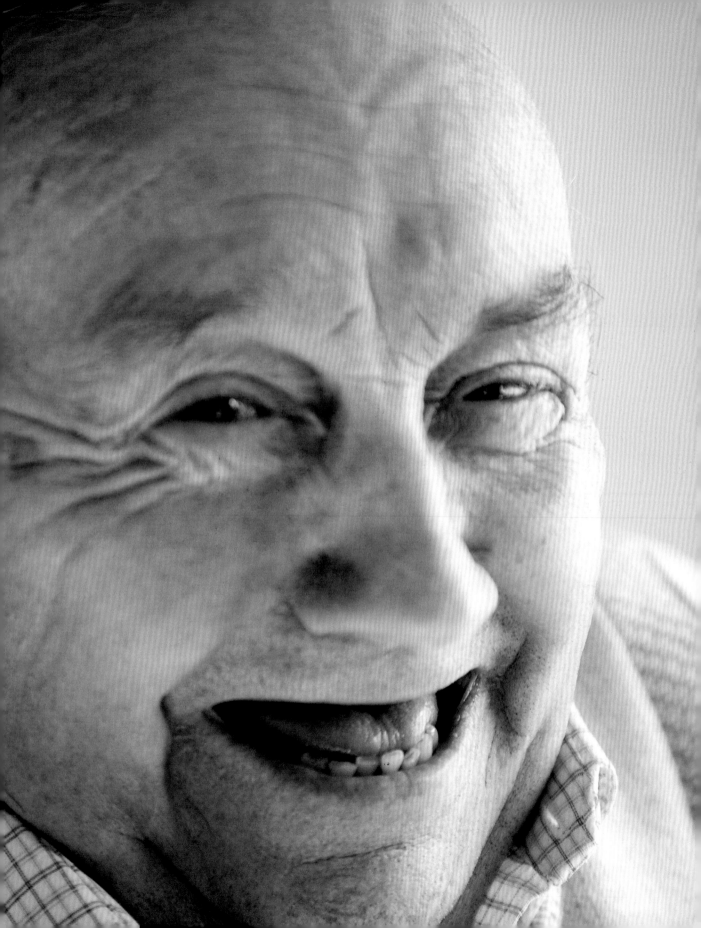

all the time,' laughs Ger. 'As the fellow says, they could have done with some precaution.'

In 1930, two major events happened in the world of greyhound racing. First, the Offaly-bred Mick the Miller won his second consecutive English Derby. And second, Malachy McKenna's wife, Agnes, gave birth to a son they called Gerard.

Ger's childhood was all about the dogs. 'I knew nothing else, only greyhounds,' he says. 'I done nothing else.' He was eight years old when he attended his first race meeting in Limerick. It was St Patrick's Day 1938 and the track had just reopened after the long winter. 'It was packed to suffocation,' he recalls. 'The crowd that night was the same as if it was the final of the Legers. There might have been 300 dogs come for the trials on the Monday, all walking up from the train station in the days before. I remember it so well because we had a bitch running and she won and I finished up with 26 shillings. I thought I was a millionaire.'

Ger went to school in Borrisokane, and later Ballyhaden, but left at the age of 14 to help his father. 'He was the boss until the day he died,' says Ger. 'He had a farm out the road and he used to buy cows and sell them at the fair in Nenagh or take them to the market in Limerick. I'd walk the cows for him. It was either that or go to school and I'd much rather be on the road.' However, an injury at school 'bucked my knee' and he was laid up in Dublin's Richmond Hospital for 19 weeks.

Ger continued to apprentice to his father until his mid-20s, when he obtained his trainer's licence. 'The shillings were scarce,' he says, 'but there was money in greyhounds.'

In 1960, Miss Josie Loughnane from Offaly arrived in Borrisokane and set up a hairdressing salon. She and Ger caught one another's eye, and married on 4 July 1962, 'the day I lost my independence', as she puts it. 'She thought I had money, d'you see?' explains Ger. 'She got an awful shock, though.'

Josie knew nothing about greyhounds when she married. She quickly became central to the business, orchestrating the transportation of dogs before all the trials and races while Ger focused on the training and kennelling.

Ger dominated the 1960s and 1970s, winning the Irish St Leger on twelve occasions, including three in a row from 1975–7. 'I was lucky enough,' he says. 'I'm not bragging or boasting or anything but I won everything. Forty-four classics, with English and Irish derbys and everything.'

One of his first and fastest dogs was Prince of Bermuda. 'He was the Master McGrath of that era,' says Ger, regarding the dog's portrait on the sitting-room wall. 'He won everything but the Derby and broke records on every track he went on. He was the first dog to break twenty-nine seconds at Shelbourne. That was the greatest moment in greyhound racing. The whole place was on fire.' Prince of Bermuda was a supremely intelligent dog, says Ger, and the only one he has had who genuinely seemed to understand what he was saying. However, he was also typical of a brilliant dog that 'never bred nothing' even though he 'got a bitch every day of the week'.

He laments the twilight of the coursing age, but understands that young lads might prefer computers to watching a hare throw a few turns in a wet field. He growls at the notion that dog fighting might still exist.

The year 1967 was a golden one, with Yanka Boy winning the St Leger at Limerick, the Cesarewitch at Navan and the Midlands Puppy Stakes at Mullingar, as well as Irish Greyhound of the Year. When Bashful Man, the second of Ger's three Irish Derby winners, sprinted home in 1973 in a time of 28.82, that was the fastest time ever recorded for a Derby final.

The English Derby had always been his goal and in 1981 the most feared name in Irish racing launched his assault with Parkdown Jet. The scenes that followed his triumph were comparable to those of an FA Cup final. He secured another English Derby in 1989 with Lartigue Note, as well as the Oaks and the Waterloo Cup. 'But I got bayt in them all a few times, too,' he points out. 'You never hear about the losers!'

Ger maintains that the greatest nights of his life were winning his Texaco Awards and winning the Irish Laurels at Curraheen Park in Cork City with his three sons by his side (he won all four of the big races in Cork that night).

Ger retired from training in 2003. Today, he and Josie live in a bungalow just outside the village of Borrisokane. They have three sons, one of whom trains greyhounds near the Rock of Cashel. The McKennas do not have a pet dog.

'The whole thing with dogs is trying to keep them fresh so that they will come out of that box as quick as they can,' says Ger. 'They were bred to hunt. That's the way they started and that's why they chase.

'Nothing is certain,' he observes. 'They say square-headed dogs are wrong, but I saw more square-headed dogs win than anything. You might be looking for a dog with straight hind legs, but I saw them cow-hocked with legs out this way and that, and still they could win.'

Ger McKenna stands with his three sons, John, Ger junior and Owen, on the night his dogs triumphed at four of the big races at Curraheen Park in Cork City in 1983. That included the Irish Laurels, which Back Garden won in a time of 29.66. (Photographer unknown)

STEVE COLLINS

Boxing

TITLES
Irish Senior Middleweight Champion, 1986
Irish Professional Middleweight Champion,
  1988
USBA Middleweight Champion, 1989
WBA Penta-Continental Middleweight
  Champion, 1993
WBO Middlewight Champion, 1994
WBO Super Middleweight Champion, 1995

RECORD
Wins: 36
Wins by KO: 21
Losses: 3

In 1990, just as 25-year-old Steve Collins was preparing to take on world middleweight champion Mike McCallum, an ABC cameraman caught up with the Dublin boxer. Steve's grandfather, John O'Rourke, was by his side, beaming with pride. 'So Grandad started showing the guy from ABC his moves. "Here's the famous O'Rourke left hook," he says, and he brings his hand down and up and clips me on the chin. "Oh my God, I'm sorry," he said, "did I hurt you?"

'"No," I said, "you didn't Grandad, but the problem is when McCallum sees what you just did, he'll know I'm open for that punch."'

McCallum won the fight and it took Steve another six years to become world champion. He says his grandfather John O'Rourke knew how to punch. He learned the hard way, in the St Vincent de Paul Orphanage in Glasnevin where he spent his childhood, before he went to work at the Guinness Brewery aged 15. John's son, Jack O'Rourke, was both an Irish middleweight and heavyweight champion in the 1960s. And, in time, John's daughter Collette would marry a Guinness-based boxer called Paschal Collins, father of Steve.

Paschal Collins was named for his uncle Patrick Gallagher, a Liberties boy who was killed at Ypres in April 1915. In one of the more poignant stories from that cataclysmic era, Patrick and his four brothers had all signed up with the British Army at the outbreak of the First World War. By 1916, all five lay dead, some upon the barbed wire coils of the Western Front, others ambushed by unseen forces in Macedonia and Basra. They left behind one sister, Annie, whom Steve knew well as 'Nan'. By her husband John Collins, Annie had five sons. She named each one after her five slain brothers.

'My father and all my Collins uncles worked in Guinness's,' says Steve. 'My dad and my uncles Terry and John were in the traffic department.' It was hot and sweaty work, loading all the hops and grain, but it gave you powerful muscles. Paschal, Steve's father, also enjoyed boxing. Indeed, he fought for the Leinster title in the first boxing match shown on Irish television. 'My mam watched it with her baby on her lap.'

Born in 1964, Steve was the third of four sons. 'My mother told me I was the only planned baby,' he winks, 'so I'm special.' They were raised in Cabra, a semi-rural suburb which sprang up on Dublin's northside after the Second World War. The countryside was close enough to inspire Steve's interest in horses. 'I was only a nipper when I started to work with the trainer Noel Chance. He was just up the road at Luttrellstown. That's where I learned to ride, taking racehorses out for some exercise.'

Steve was eight years old when he decided he was going to be world champion. The epiphany took place at the Corinthian Boxing Club, a basement gym on Gardiner Street, when he won a junior tournament. 'I remember going down clear as if it was last week, the guys walking around watching the timing, another guy with his thumb over a lemonade bottle spilling water to keep the dust down . . . the buzz I got winning that day is still with me.'

By the time *Rocky* hit the silver screen in 1976, the 11 year old was hell-bent on boxing. But his father urged him to get a trade first. Five years later, when Steve was seventeen, Paschal Collins went for his regular jog. He suffered a massive heart attack in the Phoenix Park and never returned home. Steve left school to start as an apprentice electrician at the Guinness Brewery.

Young Steve wanted to be a heavyweight champion but he wasn't big enough. 'I kept on eating and eating so I'd get big. I figured I'd be a short and stocky heavyweight like Rocky Marciano.' By the age of seventeen, he had three titles, including heavyweight, under his belt. He began sparring with Joe Christle. 'That was a defining moment for me. Joe was a proper heavyweight and he didn't take it easy on me. He beat [Frank] Bruno. I thought, I'm too small for this, and I dropped down to light heavyweight in weeks.'

By the time he turned professional in 1986, Steve had won amateur Irish titles at middleweight, light heavyweight and heavyweight. He was also middleweight champion of Ireland. After a sparring session with Christle's US-trained brother Terry, he decided the time had come to go to America and turn pro.

Soon the 21 year old was working out at the Petronelli Brothers Gym in Brockton, Massachusetts, alongside his icon, world champion Marvin Hagler. 'I worked my way up and eventually, after a few years, I was top dog . . . even Marvin said I was top dog.'

In 1988, Steve won the Irish professional middleweight title in Boston. He enjoyed a run of 16 successive victories, including the USA middleweight title, before he was outpointed over 12 rounds in the WBA world middleweight title in Boston in 1990.

He moved to Belfast, under the management of Barney Eastwood, and then joined Barry Hearn's Matchroom Sport in England. In 1994, Steve defeated Chris Pyatt to secure the WBO middleweight belt.

The following year he relinquished this title without a defence and moved up to super middleweight. In March 1995, he embarked on perhaps the finest fight of his career, against the previously unbeaten world champion Chris Eubank. When Steve won, Eubank accused him of playing mind games. 'But I had the hunger to beat him,' says Steve. 'You have to have the hunger to succeed.'

The new world champion whirled his Reyes-clad fists to defend his title seven successive times, including a second meeting with Eubank at Millstreet in Cork and two fights against Nigel Benn. On the eve of his showdown with Benn, he famously told *The Sun* that Readymix Concrete had offered to sponsor his chin.

The Celtic Warrior, as he became known, fought his last professional fight in 1997, annihilating his opponent. Injury obliged him to step down shortly afterwards and he handed in his title. On doctors' orders, he officially retired in 1999. 'Nobody ever knocked me out,' he says. 'And nor are they ever going to.'

Steve was formerly based in Bangor, Co. Down, with his then wife and their children. He now lives on a 55-acre farm just outside the old Roman town of St Albans, England, with his second wife Donna. He had a cameo in Guy Ritchie's *Lock, Stock and Two Smoking Barrels*, as well as U2's video for 'Sweetest Thing'. He managed and coached in Ireland for a while, before returning to the UK. He and his brother Paschal, also a former boxing pro, have lately opened a gym in Corduff which he hopes will boost sporting ambitions in the area.

'Life is good,' he says. 'I have five children, all healthy, clever and great characters. I'm very lucky. I was rearing sheep until a year ago but it was too hard work. They're escapologists! My passion has always been my horses. The week I retired, I bought my hunter. I hunt twice a week. I just got another horse so I might go three times.' He hunts with the Pytchley Hunt 'and anyone else who will have me' and plays a prominent role as manager of the St Albans Polo Club. He has also ridden in several races, including a ride at Fairyhouse. 'Riding out, mucking out, breaking the ice in the troughs . . . that's what keeps me fit these days.'

Steve Collins swings a left hook at Nigel Benn during the Benn v. Collins rematch at the Nynex Arena in Manchester in 1996. Benn, who gave up boxing after the fight, retired at the end of the sixth round and Steve retained the WBO super middleweight title.
(© John Gichigi/Allsport, Getty Images)

MICHAEL CARRUTH

Boxing

TITLES
Irish Lightweight Champion, 1987, 1988
Irish Light Welterweight Champion, 1990
Irish Welterweight Champion, 1992
WAA Welterweight Champion, 1998

RECORD:
Wins: 18
Wins by KO: 11
Losses: 3

MEDALS
Olympics, 1992, gold
World Amateur Championships, 1989,
  bronze

AWARDS
Texaco Sportstar Award, 1992
Irish Amateur Boxing Association Hall
  of Fame, 2010

'We started in Scotland but they fecked us out so we became mercenaries and we fought for whoever had the most money, so things haven't really changed.' Retired army sergeant Michael Carruth leans back against the ropes of the Drimnagh Boxing Club and smiles. 'I believe we were from Norway originally,' he adds.

Nearly 20 years after his show-stopping Olympic gold, Ireland's most successful amateur boxer is preparing himself for an evening's workout with the young gents from the inner city who are gathered here to hone their fighting skills and enjoy a little sparring. The room echoes with the sound of rubber soles squeaking and pounding upon the floor, as nine punchbags are smacked by rolling fists that bristle with cocksure confidence. Along the walls are photographic portraits of boxing icons like Ali and McGuigan, mixed with those of club stalwarts like Martin Doran and Paul Griffin. A glass-fronted cabinet in the corner contains the impressive silverware the club has scooped in its 40 years of service.

Michael's father, Austin 'Aussie' Carruth, has been one of the most enthusiastic supporters of the Drimnagh BC since it opened. Aussie's grandfather William Carruth was a Protestant carpenter from Co. Tyrone born in 1885. During his early 20s, he and his wife Annie lived in Co. Fermanagh, where their first son Billy was born. By the time their second son Victor was born in 1909, they were living at 31 Usher's Quay in Dublin. Billy, the eldest son, was Aussie's father and Michael's grandfather. He worked as a carpenter, builder and tradesman in Dublin. 'He was born in the north so they used to call him "Billy the Brit",' laughs Michael.

Protestant or not, Billy soon became romantically entwined with Miss Bridget Gaffney, a young Catholic woman from the Thomas Street area of Dublin. In November 1922, her brother John Gaffney was one of four IRA men executed in Kilmainham Jail on the orders of the 26-county Irish Free State government. Their dubious charge was possession of a revolver. 'They arrested them, gave them back their arms on the street and then rearrested them again,' says Michael.

Billy and Bridget lived in Cabra, where they raised their two sons and three daughters as Catholics. The teenage Aussie went to live with Bridget's mother, Granny Gaffney, whose husband had since died. Neighbours referred to him as Aussie Gaffney. Aussie liked to box and, when he was 13, he joined the St Francis Boxing Club. The club was run by Martin Humpston and Aussie began spending time with Mr Humpston's sons, including Martin Humpston Jr, who became Ireland's first light middleweight champion in 1951 and later served as a much-admired trainer at Coventry's Bell Green club.

'And then one day, when he was 14 or 15 years old, my dad came to the Humpston house and he saw this young girl called Joan, who was a sister of the brothers he was hanging out with. So he started courting her and, well, now they're both 76 and they've been married 53 years. Her dad used to call him "Carruth" all the time.'

Like his father, Aussie became a builder. He and Joan settled in Greenhills, where they had ten children. 'All ten of us were married and all ten of us are still married. That's something my mother and father are immensely proud of in this day, when people get separated if they have a fight over what colour the fecking duvet on the bed should be. None of us emigrated. And we're very close-knit. No matter what goes wrong in a family, it can be fixed. If you owe a few bob, you can find it. If it's emotional, talk about it. There's nothing unfixable.'

Michael was one of triplets born in 1967, towards the younger end of those ten children. 'Yeah, yeah, we used to switch around and do all those tricks,' he says. The triplets left school after their Junior Certificate. William became an apprentice electrician, Martin joined a carpet company and Michael enlisted with the 2nd Infantry Battalion of the Irish Army and moved to Cathal Brugha Barracks in Rathmines.

'I joined for employment,' he says, 'but it turned out to be the best move I ever made. I was full-time fighting and training all day. You couldn't ask for better. They transferred me into the gym and gave me leave to go to all these games and championships. I still had to do my regimental duties but I got looked after because I was boxing for Ireland and I was representing the Defence Forces.'

In 1988, he went to the Seoul Olympics but was beaten in his second fight. 'I was dropped for the first and only time in my life. I got up and the fight was over.' There was no sympathy when he returned to the barracks. 'The amount of slagging I got. "You lost in the Olympics, ya bleeding waster!" Those comments hurt as much as any punch. I had to get back, which I done, and then I went and won the bloody thing!'

In 1992, five months after his marriage, Michael returned to box at the Barcelona Olympics. With Aussie coaching him, the young freckle-faced corporal from Drimnagh beat Juan Hernández of Cuba 13–10 to become the first Irishman since Ronnie Delany to win gold. 'To be honest, the lads in the battalion were immensely proud. I was flying the flag for them when I won the gold. My medal was their medal and still is.'

Michael broke both his hands during the Barcelona win and took some time out to consider his career. 'People were telling me to do this and that. I didn't know what I wanted to do. I was 25 years old and I was basically being told to give up being an amateur because I had won Olympic gold. I would have stayed amateur if anyone had made me that offer. But they didn't. So I left the army and turned professional in 1994.'

He did not particularly enjoy professional boxing and retired in 2000 with a pro-record of 18–3–0. He then began coaching alongside his father at the Drimnagh BC. (Father and son were, uniquely, inducted alongside one another into the Irish Amateur Boxing Association Hall of Fame in 2010.) 'This is my army now,' he says. 'This boxing club is what I live for. I come here every night to train these kids. Boxing has a way of humbling people when they get too big for their boots. Just listen to the slagging I'm getting, standing for photographs with you. "Ya bleedin' poser," and all. Little blaggards, half of them. But if I can make one of them a champion . . . I asked my da, "D'you think I'll be as good a coach as you?" and he said, "Yeah, but you'll have to win two Olympic golds to be better than me."'

In 1998, former Irish army soldier and Olympic gold medallist Michael Carruth won the World Athletic Association welterweight title with a one-point victory over Glasgow's Scott Dixon at the National Basketball Arena in Tallaght. (© Ray Lohan/ Sportsfile)

BARRY McGUIGAN

Boxing

TITLES
All-Ireland Juvenile Champion, 1976
All-Ireland Senior Champion, 1978–79
British Featherweight Champion, 1983
European Featherweight Champion, 1983
WBA Featherweight Champion, 1985

MEDALS
Commonwealth Games, 1978, gold

RECORD
Wins: 32
Wins by KO: 28
Losses: 3

AWARDS
BBC Sports Personality of the Year, 1985
MBE, 1986 (accepted 1994)
World Boxing Hall of Fame, 2002
RTÉ/Irish Sports Council Hall of Fame, 2004
International Boxing Hall of Fame, 2005

Silence swooped across the sun-drenched Monaghan field. The crowd drew their breath; the straw bales they sat upon inched a little closer to the stage. The band began to strum guitars and patter on drums. And then Barry McGuigan strolled into the sunlight, plucked a microphone from its stand and launched into 'Mustang Sally'. It was the Flat Lake Festival 2010 and, as the first couples began to shimmy up for a dance, everyone agreed that the Clones Cyclone was in fine voice.

The singing thing is genetic. Barry's grandfather James McGuigan, who came from Red Bog, near Draperstown, Co. Derry, was a ballad singer who frequently entertained the crowds at St Joseph's Hall in Clones during the 1930s and 1940s. He found work as a railwayman in Co. Tyrone, where he also found his wife, Mary McShane of Pomeroy. In 1923, the couple moved across the new border to Clones, Co. Monaghan, in the Irish Free State, where James worked as a signalman until the closure of the railway in 1960.

Their son Pat McGuigan, Barry's late father, became a household name across Ireland when he came fourth in the 1968 Eurovision Song Contest with his ballad 'Chance of a Lifetime'. The song went on to top the Irish charts.

Pat's wife Katie was a daughter of Johnny Rooney, an egg factory worker from Clones, and his wife Josephine McCaul. Katie ran a grocery shop on The Diamond in Clones for

25 years, ably assisted by her father until his death in 1983. The shop is now a hairdresser's salon run by Sharon, Katie's eldest daughter.

Katie was working in the shop the night her son Finbar Patrick McGuigan conquered the world. Understandably she's never been a great fan of watching other men pummel their fists into her son's face.

But Pat was there. In fact, the whole world knew he was there because shortly before the match began, he sang 'Danny Boy' live from the ring at Loftus Road Football Stadium in west London. It was 8 June 1985, the night 24-year-old Barry McGuigan of Clones dropped reigning champion Eusebio Pedroza of Panama in the seventh round to become the World Boxing Association's world featherweight champion.

Ireland erupted. The country needed heroes and the 5 ft 6 in. mustachioed knockout specialist from Clones was now the most popular Irishman to step into the ring since Rinty Monaghan back in the 1940s. Thousands turned out on the streets of Belfast and Dublin to greet Barry and his wife Sandra upon their return from victory. That December he became the first Irishman to win the coveted BBC Sports Personality of the Year.

When asked what inspired him to box, Barry likes to quote Ernest Hemingway, who described boxing as 'the most honest conversation two men can have'. Barry is good at honesty. His triumph on the international stage took place at a time when the Troubles in Ulster were about as bitter and bloody as they ever were. But Barry himself remained defiantly non-political, repeatedly stating that his success was Ireland's success, to be shared by all Irish people north and south of the border. His determination to reject religious divides was undoubtedly cemented by the fact that while he was a Catholic, his wife was Protestant. Perhaps the most outward display of his penchant for diplomacy was his decision to use the colours of the UN flag of peace for his shorts.

Barry's boxing career began when he and some pals started sparring for fun in Clones. His father had some experience of the sport, having trained at the Clones Amateur Boxing Club. At the age of 12, Barry convinced his father to bring him to the Wattlebridge ABC near the border.

He then advanced to the Smithborough ABC in Co. Monaghan, where he proved himself an exceptional amateur. In 1977, the 16 year old won the All-Ireland Juvenile Championship. The following year he won the Ulster and Irish senior titles, and a gold for Northern Ireland at the Commonwealth Games in Edmonton. In 1978, he captained the Irish boxing team at the Moscow Olympics, controversially going out in the penultimate round before the medal stage.

In 1981, Barry's professional career began in Dublin when he knocked out Selwyn Bell in the second round. The following year, he won eight fights, seven by knockouts. However, amongst those he knocked out was Young Ali, a Nigerian boxer who subsequently fell into a six-month coma and died. The tragedy pulled Barry into a psychological dark cloud and he strongly considered retiring. 'It was a very difficult time,' he says, 'and it took a long time to get over it. But I didn't have any other form of income. I had dedicated my whole life to boxing and I had to make a choice and that choice was to continue boxing.'

He returned to the ring in 1983 and won five fights in a row. He won the European featherweight belt in November that year, knocking out Italian Valerio Nati in the sixth round.

He gradually worked his way up the world rankings during 1984, winning six contests in a row by knockout. The following year, he became world featherweight champion when he beat the legendary Pedroza, who had held the title for more than seven years.

After two successful defences in Belfast and Dublin, Barry's reign came to an abrupt end in the blazing Las Vegas sunshine when the Texan boxer Stevie 'Super Kid' Cruz beat him on points over fifteen rounds on 23 June 1986. Barry was rushed to hospital after the match with severe dehydration.

Defeat, poor health and the sudden death of his father prompted him to take a two-year break from the ring. He returned in 1988, beating two former world title challengers, but retired permanently after losing on a cut-eye stoppage to former European champion Jim McDonnell in May 1989.

Barry spent two years training Daniel Day-Lewis to professional fighting standards for the 1997 Jim Sheridan-directed movie *The Boxer* and he also choreographed all the fight scenes. The film was nominated for three Golden Globe Awards.

In the twenty-first century, it is arguable that Barry is as well known for his mashed potato and his band as anything. Few boxers have cultivated a more diverse post-ring career. In 2007, he was crowned winner of ITV's hugely successful *Hell's Kitchen*. He currently works as a boxing commentator for ITV and writes a weekly column for the *Daily Mirror*. He tried his hand at acting, appearing in the movie *Malicious Intent* in

On 15 February 1986, 6,500 fans squeezed into the RDS Simmonscourt Pavilion in Dublin to watch 'Clones Cyclone' Barry McGuigan successfully defend his title against Danilo Cabrera. It was the first world championship bout held in Dublin since 1923. (© Ray McManus/Sportsfile)

2000. His band frequently appears at the Flat Lake Festival near Clones and has also performed at the Albert Hall with Paul Carrack, formerly of Squeeze and Mike and the Mechanics.

In November 2009, he launched the inaugural Barry McGuigan Boxing Academy, aimed at helping young people achieve their academic and sporting goals, and seeking to encourage students struggling to stay in the education system. The academy addresses Barry's oft-stated concerns about the welfare and education of boxers, particularly those who become so obsessed with becoming a champion that, when they fail, they are left depressed and abandoned. Barry urges upcoming boxers to work on their other skills and master a trade to ensure they have something to fall back on.

Barry lives in Whitstable in Kent with Sandra, his wife of 29 years. They have four children, Blain, Danika, Jake and Shane. In 1997, Danika was diagnosed with leukaemia. With the aid of the CLIC (Cancer and Leukaemia in Childhood) Sargent nurses, she completely recovered. Barry and Sandra have both been active as patrons of the children's cancer charity ever since. 'It is immensely gratifying for us, as they helped save our daughter's life,' he says.

DONNACHA O'DEA

Swimming and Poker

Swimming
IRISH NATIONAL RECORDS
Freestyle: 100 m, 200 m, 400 m, 800 m,
    1,500 m
Butterfly: 100 m, 200 m
Individual medley: 400 m

AWARDS
European Poker Players' Hall of Fame

Poker
WORLD SERIES OF POKER
Bracelet, 1998
Money finishes: 23
Highest ITM Main Event finish: 6th, 1983

Shortly after the death of the actor Denis O'Dea in 1978, his fellow thespian Gabriel Fallon recalled an encounter with Seán Lemass. 'Take my advice,' counselled the former Taoiseach. 'Never play poker with Denis O'Dea. That chap plays from the cellar up!'

Mr Lemass was a regular at the poker table in the O'Dea family home in the Dublin suburb of Rathgar. Denis mastered the game in the Kenyan jungles while filming *Mogambo* with Clark Gable and Grace Kelly. Before the eight players took their seats, he and his young son Donnacha would lay the baize upon the dining-room table and prepare the chips. Donnacha was allowed to stay and watch for the first half-hour. Those short episodes sowed the seeds of poker-lust in the boy, rather to the dismay of his mother, the actress Siobhán McKenna.

An exquisite pencil portrait of Siobhán McKenna adorns the wall of Donnacha's Dalkey home. Born close to Belfast's Falls Road in 1923, Siobhán was the daughter of Eoghan McKenna, an academic from Cork City then teaching maths at Queen's University, Belfast. In 1928, Eoghan was appointed professor of maths at University College Galway and the family moved west. Always different, young Siobhán was expelled from the Dominican convent in Galway City after an episode involving a nun and a bag of flour. She went on to become arguably the finest stage actress Ireland has yet produced.

In 1946, two years after she joined the Abbey Theatre, Siobhán married Denis O'Dea. Born in 1903, Denis was, like many actors of his generation, an ardent Republican from his teenage years, befriending Lady Gregory while working as a reporter in Sligo during

the early part of the War of Independence. This prompted something of a fall-out with his father, Michael O'Dea, an officer in the Royal Irish Constabulary. During the Irish Civil War, Denis narrowly escaped arrest when the Free State soldier assigned to frisk him transpired to be an old school friend. Feeling the butt of Denis's hidden gun, the soldier quietly said, 'You had better go home now.' Denis joined the Abbey in the 1920s and went on to star in a number of Hollywood movies, most notably as the inspector in pursuit of James Mason in *Odd Man Out*.

Born in 1948, Donnacha was Denis and Siobhán's only child. He grew up in Dublin and was educated first at the Gaelscoil (or Irish-language school) in Blackrock and later at the Christian Brothers School on Synge Street. At the latter establishment he developed into a swimmer of Olympic stature, becoming the greatest Irish swimmer of the 1960s.

'My father was very into fishing and often took me out on boats on the Corrib, or for walks along the riverbanks. He wanted to be able to relax knowing that I could swim so he took me to the Tara Street Baths in Dublin when I was four years old and taught me how to swim. He was always at me to swim! When we went down to the sea at Booterstown and I wanted to play, he'd say, "Swim from here to there first and then you can mess around."'

In 1956, both Siobhán and Denis won roles in two separate plays on Broadway and the family relocated to New York for six months. Seven-year-old Donnacha took full advantage to swim in the local pool and was taught how to crawl properly. Three years later, he entered the school gala at Synge Street and won the race. He was invited to join the local Club Sná Colmcille and began to swim on a more regular basis.

The following year, Donnacha's ascent began when he won two Under-14s Leinster championships, and then scooped the Irish 1,500 m freestyle at the Blackrock Baths. In 1963, he won his first seniors title, winning the Men's 400 m freestyle at the Grove Baths in Belfast. 'I had never competed against guys from the north before,' he says. 'They looked like giants.'

In 1965, the year his mother played Dr Zhivago's mother-in-law in David Lean's epic, 16-year-old Donnacha O'Dea broke the barrier to become the first Irishman to swim 100 m in less than a minute. 'I didn't even think about breaking it,' he says. 'It was a big deal in Irish swimming but I was sort of oblivious to it until the night.'

Thereafter he dominated Irish swimming, at one time holding all five of Ireland's senior freestyle titles – 100, 200, 400, 800 and 1,500 – as well as the two butterfly titles and the individual medley. 'I did a bit of a Michael Phelps on it all,' he laughs, referring to the American swimmer who presently holds 14 Olympic gold medals.

His zest was somewhat complicated by the lack of infrastructure. The biggest pool in the city was the 25 m pool that Guinness had opened for its employees. The gate man was under strict instructions from the union not to let any non-Guinness workers in. 'So I asked my father to ask Seán Lemass to see if he could have a word with the MD of Guinness to let me train there! My father said, "God, I'd prefer to save that favour for when you murder somebody . . . that's a very big one."'

One way or another, the request went through and ultimately Donnacha was allowed to train at Guinness's early in the morning while the pool was being cleaned. He also became affiliated with the Guinness Swimming Club, which gave him some much-needed competition.

In 1968, four weeks before he was due at the Olympic Games in Mexico City, Donnacha twisted his ankle on some steps. While he nonetheless won his race in the National Championships that followed, the altitude in Mexico got the better of him. He continued to swim on his return from Mexico, representing Ireland at the European Championships in Utrecht and Barcelona. However, while he won the two butterflys and the individual medley at the National Championships in 1972, his time was not sufficient for him to qualify for the Munich Olympics. He retired from swimming at the age of 24.

Meanwhile, a genetic habit had taken hold and it wasn't acting. 'My parents never wanted me to act. They had seen so many of their colleagues struggling to make a living and they thought it was a very tough profession. But I don't think my mother exactly wanted me to be a poker player either!'

Donnacha learned the game watching his father, Lemass and others playing in his family home. While his academic career began to peter out – he was at both University College Dublin and Trinity College Dublin – he had taken a deeper interest in the game.

Having observed those long poker sessions at his family home during his childhood, Donnacha developed his interest while at university in Dublin during the 1960s. 'My father always said it's not how much you win, its just that you win. He was a very disciplined

Donnacha O'Dea began displaying his record-breaking tactics at the 1964 Irish swimming championships at Butlins holiday camp in Mosney, Co. Meath. During the contest, the fifteen year old won nine gold medals and established four new Irish records. Here he is presented with the trophy for the 400 m individual medley. (Photographer unknown)

player, but he told me he once had a losing streak when his game went off the boil for 18 months. It made a huge impression on me that such a steady Eddie player could get unlucky for 18 months. I always kept that at the back of my mind.'

'The Don', as he became known, made his first appearance at the World Series of Poker tournament in Las Vegas in 1982. The following year, he nearly won a WSOP bracelet in the $1,000 limit hold 'em event. He had to wait until 1998 for that win, when he defeated two-time world champion Johnny Chan in pot limit Omaha.

He finished fourth in the Grand Final of the *Late Night Poker* television programme in 2002 and won the 2004 Poker Million tournament. In December 2008, Donnacha's son Eoghan was very unlucky not to win the same tournament, coming second. However, there was some consolation as Eoghan won $300,000 online that very week.

The poker world is changing rapidly. 'It's gone crazy,' says Donnacha. 'There's 8,000 players at the main event in Las Vegas now, but they've kept the entry fee at $10,000. To try and hope to win it is a total dream. The bookies bet 1,000–1 the field.'

Most of the change is Internet-related. 'The dominant players now are guys of 21 or 22 years who you've never heard of. They've just played so many hands on the Internet! If I go into a casino, they deal me thirty hands an hour so if I stay ten hours, that's three hundred hands. But on the Internet, they'll get about seventy-five hands an hour and these guys are playing six or seven games at the same time. They don't even go to a casino, but in one year they can play as much poker as I did in twenty.

'The last poker event I went to was at a ski resort in Austria,' he says. 'I love skiing so that was perfect. Ski all day, off the slopes, quick shower and into the cash game. Really nice! I'll certainly do that one again.'

JESSIE HARRINGTON

Three-Day Eventing and Horse Racing

EVENTING HIGHLIGHTS
Badminton Trials, 1966, 1967, 1968, 1980,
    1981, 1982, 1983
European Championships, 1967, 1981, 1983
Substitute Olympics, 1980
World Championships, 1982
Los Angeles Olympics, 1984

MAJOR WINS AS TRAINER
Aintree
Melling Chase: 2

Cheltenham
Queen Mother Champion Chase: 2
Champion Bumper: 1
Arkle Challenge Trophy: 1
County Hurdle: 1
Grand Annual Handicap Chase: 1

Curragh
Solonaway Stakes: 2
C.L. Weld Park Stakes: 1
Beresford Stakes: 1

Down Royal
Ulster Derby: 1

Fairyhouse
Novice Hurdle: 2
Handicap Hurdle: 1

Galway
Galway Hurdle: 1

Gowran Park
Champion Chase: 3
Trial Hurdle: 1

Leopardstown
December Festival Hurdle: 2
MCR Hurdle: 2
Arkle Novice Chase: 2
Irish Champion Hurdle: 1
Handicap Chase: 1
Dr P.J. Moriarty Novice Chase: 1
Synergy Security Services Novice Hurdle: 2
Paddy Power Dial-A-Bet Chase: 2

Punchestown
Champion Hurdle: 2
Champion Chase: 1
Novice Chase: 2
Champion Novice Hurdle: 2
Morgiana Hurdle: 1
Novice Handicap Chase: 1

Sandown Park
Tingle Creek Chase: 2
William Hill Handicap Hurdle: 1

Uttoxeter
Midlands Grand National: 2

In the spring of 1191, a fleet of 100 ships, carrying 8,000 soldiers of Christ, arrived on the Mediterranean coast north of Jerusalem and laid siege to the Muslim port of Acre. Amongst those assembled warriors was Robert Fowler of Foxley, Buckinghamshire, who rode at the head of a troop of highly skilled archers. When his bowmen successfully repelled an ambush by the infidels, Robert was knighted by Richard the Lionheart, King of England.

In 1991, precisely 800 years later, Sir Robert's direct descendant Jessie Harrington (née Fowler) began to take on infidels of a somewhat tweedier nature when she opened her account as a National Hunt trainer.

Over the ensuing two decades, Jessie has established herself as the leading woman trainer in Ireland. Her stables at Commonstown Stud, Moone, Co. Kildare, are responsible for several iconic horses, headed up by the inestimable Moscow Flyer, winner of the Arkle and the Queen Mother Champion Chase at successive Cheltenham Festivals, as well as such high-class performers as Space Trucker, Dance Beat, Spirit Leader and Macs Joy.

The Fowler family, descendants of the crusading archer, are believed to have arrived in Ireland in the fourteenth century and made their mark as churchmen. Robert Fowler, a private chaplain to George II, became Archbishop of Dublin and was elected first president of the Order of St Patrick.

By the late eighteenth century, they were living at Rahinston, near Summerhill, Co. Meath, where they became stalwarts of the Meath Hunt, the smartest pack in Ireland. They were breeding horses on their 850-acre farm by the time Empress Sisi of the Austro-Hungarian Empire visited Ireland in 1879. Sisi apparently took a liking to a horse belonging to Jessie's great-aunt Louisa Fowler. But when Louisa's father got wind of her interest, he snorted, 'I'm not going to have any damned empress buying my daughter's horse.'

Known as 'the Brig', Bryan Fowler, Jessie's father, was a decorated army officer, Master of the Meath foxhounds and a member of the Irish National Hunt Steeplechase Committee. He was also on the British polo team that won silver at the 1936 Olympics and, in 1944, he married Mary Nickalls, daughter of another great English polo champion, Colonel Cecil Nickalls.

Under the Brig's careful tuition, their two children, John and Jessie, effectively grew up in the saddle and were perpetually out riding, eventing, hunting and trotting about at pony clubs, Mosney gymkhanas and the Navan Agricultural Show.

In 1957, the Brig relocated his family to Rahinston when he succeeded to the farm upon the death of a centenarian uncle. During his tenure, the estate was the venue every April for the Meath Hunt and Tara Harriers Point-to-Point.

In April 1958, 11-year-old Jessie Fowler was on the victorious team when the Meath Hunt won the All-Ireland Pony Club Championships at Castletown House in Celbridge. Three years later, the fourteen year old won the Under-17s title at the Pony Club Championships in Burley-on-the–Hill in Oakham, England.

In 1966, the willowy beauty from Co. Meath was selected as one of five Irish riders to compete at the international three-day event at Badminton in England. She was due to ride her father's nine-year-old gelding, Gold Buck. The Irish press considered them 'a very steady and capable combination', but unfortunately the event was cancelled due to bad weather.

In 1967, Jessie and John became the first brother and sister to be on the same team when they represented Ireland at the European Eventing Championships in Punchestown. The following year John rode for Ireland at the Mexico Olympics.

Jessie returned to the Badminton trials in 1967 and 1968, and again every year from 1980 to 1983. She rates her third place in 1983 (on Amoy, who was bred by her father) as the most memorable moment of her eventing career. She also represented Ireland at the European Championships in 1967, 1981 and 1983, the Substitute Olympics at Fontainebleau in 1980, the World Championships in Luhmühlen in 1982, and the Los Angeles Olympics in 1984.

In August 1968, Jessie married the late David Lloyd, with whom she had a son, James, and daughter, Tara. The couple subsequently divorced and in 1976, she married bloodstock agent Johnny Harrington, with whom she has two daughters, Emma and Kate.

By the late 1980s, Jessie's interest in riding horses had extended to training them. She obtained her trainer's licence in 1991 and saddled her first winner in Leopardstown later that year. In 1994, she sent Oh So Grumpy stomping home to victory in the keenly contested Galway Hurdle. It was the first time a woman trainer had won the race and the victory brought considerable attention to the 100-acre yard at Commonstown as owners began to consider the hitherto undreamed of possibility of a successful woman trainer. But even then, when prospective owners phoned the Harringtons, they would often automatically ask to speak to Johnny.

The calls began to come through for Jessie herself when the home-bred Space Trucker, another of her early stars, ended up being more successful than the Hollywood movie for which he was named. He recorded 15 wins between 1995 and 2002, including the 1999 Grand Annual Handicap Chase at Cheltenham. 'A win anywhere is good,' says Jessie, 'but a win at Cheltenham with a horse you've bred and trained from scratch is very special indeed.'

More recent stars include Spirit Leader, who completed a notable treble of big handicap hurdle successes during the 2002–03 season and the much loved Macs Joy, the 2005 AIG Champion Hurdler of Ireland, who tragically broke a leg at Cheltenham in 2007 and had to be destroyed. Cork All Star's victory in the Festival Bumper in 2007 provided Jessie with her seventh Cheltenham win.

However, the horse with which Jessie will forever be associated is Moscow Flyer, a steed so popular that a book Jessie wrote about him became a bestseller. His wins include the Arkle Chase at the 2002 Cheltenham Festival and his seven-length victory in the 2003 Queen Mother Champion Chase. Two years later, 'The Flyer' regained the Champion Chase in style, before adding the Melling Chase at Aintree to his scalp collection. By the time the flamboyant gelding retired in 2006, he had won 26 of his 44 starts, including 13 wins at Grade 1 level, and brought in just under €1,750,000 in prize money. At the 2007 Punchestown Festival, Jessie's daughter Kate managed to gallop the old warrior to a heroic triumph in the annual charity race.

Tragedy struck in December 2008 when Jessie's brother John was killed in a freak accident at Rahinston. He had been one of the leading amateur riders of his generation, partnering 243 winners under rules and more than 200 in point-to-points, including back-to-back wins in the National Hunt Chase at Cheltenham. As a trainer, he won the 1989 Irish Grand National with Maid of Money and the 1997 Melling Chase with Opera Hat. The John Fowler Memorial Mares' Chase at Fairyhouse is now run annually in his memory.

A famously hard worker, Jessie continues to conduct a busy yard with 80 horses and 30 employees. She has also shown her prowess on the flat, winning the Solonaway Stakes twice with Jumbajukiba in 2007 and 2008, and the 2008 Ulster Derby with Fantoche. At the 2010 Punchestown Festival, her 33–1 outsider Auspicious Outlook seized the INH Flat Race while 10–1 shot Chasing Cars romped home to a ten-length victory in the Novice Handicap Chase.

Pictured in 2000 at her stud farm in Moone, Co. Kildare, Jessie Harrington stands beside Have Merci, owned and bred by Ronnie Wood of the Rolling Stones. (© Matt Browne/Sportsfile)

PADDY MULLINS

Horse Racing

MAJOR WINS AS TRAINER

Aintree
Aintree Hurdle: 1

Auteuil
French Champion Hurdle (Grande Course
  de Haies): 1

Cheltenham
Gold Cup: 1
Champion Hurdle: 1
National Hunt Chase: 2
Sun Alliance Novices' Hurdle: 1
Novices' Chase: 1
Cleeve Hurdle: 1

Curragh
Irish Oaks: 1

Fairyhouse
Irish Grand National: 4
Royal Bond Novice Hurdle: 1

Galway
Galway Plate: 3
Galway Hurdle: 4

Gowran Park
Thyestes Chase: 1

Kempton Park
Ladbrokes Christmas Hurdle: 1

Leopardstown
Irish Champion Hurdle: 2
Arkle Novice Chase: 3
MCR Hurdle: 2
December Festival Hurdle: 6
Deloitte Novice Hurdle: 2

Newmarket
Champion Stakes: 1

Punchestown
Champion Four-Year-Old Hurdle: 4
Champion Novice Hurdle: 2

AWARDS
Texaco Sportstars Award, 1984
Texaco Sportstars Hall of Fame, 2003

'And the mare is beginning to get up!' With those seven words, racing commentator Peter O'Sullevan sent a shiver of delicious anticipation up a million spines across Ireland and Britain. Dawn Run, arguably the most outstanding filly of the 1980s, was accelerating to the finish line of the 1986 Cheltenham Gold Cup under Jonjo O'Neill.

Within seconds of Mr O'Sullevan's words, Dawn Run had made turf history and become the first horse to win the Champion Hurdle and the Gold Cup. It was the biggest Gold Cup prize ever raced for and the biggest crowd Cheltenham had yet known.

Her win was something of a coup for her trainer Paddy Mullins, dubbed the quiet man of Irish racing by the British press. He had been given the Cork-born mare to train by her owner, the redoubtable Charmain Hill, when she was a three year old. Paddy had educated her in the art of the Bumper and in 1983 she won the Novices' Hurdle at Aintree. The following year, she became the Queen of the Champion Hurdle when she won an extraordinary hat-trick of the Irish, English and French Champion Hurdles. Paddy's son Tony rode her on the latter occasion, taking her straight to the front and holding her there for a jaw-dropping three miles and one and a half furlongs, to win by six lengths.

Paddy's team at the Doninga Stables in Goresbridge, Co. Kilkenny, nursed her back from a sprained tendon over the course of 1985. And in 1986, she thrust ahead to score the Gold Cup in what is considered one of the greatest races of all time. Her success was made all the more dramatic by the Queen of Cheltenham's sudden death that summer following a horrific fall in the French Champion Hurdle. It was a profoundly sad day for everyone at the Mullins yard.

Paddy's grandfather James Mullins was born in 1860 and farmed near Graiguenamanagh, Co. Kilkenny. When the racecourse at Gowran Park was founded in 1914, he was one of the original directors. A wood stood at each corner of the new course, planted by the Annaly family who owned the land. The woods were rather prophetically shaped as a heart, a club, a diamond and a spade respectively.

James and his wife Mary Anne had thirteen children, of whom eight survived. Their son William, or Willie, was born in 1889 and relocated his family to Doninga, just outside Goresbridge, on Christmas Eve 1923. Amongst those who moved with him was his five-year-old son Paddy. And that house is the same long, low white farmhouse where Paddy and his wife Maureen live today.

At its peak, Doninga was the biggest National Hunt yard in Ireland, and Paddy was the country's most successful National Hunt trainer.

His childhood was very much an equestrian one. His father was Joint Master, with Dr O'Brien, of the Mount Loftus Harriers and Paddy was their whipper-in for most of the 1940s. He gradually progressed from pony clubs to showjumping to point-to-points. As an amateur, he won 25 point-to-points and a further 14 times under rules, on the flat, over hurdles and in chases.

From 1940 to 1953, Paddy worked as assistant trainer to his father. In April 1953, just four months after he took over his father's licence, he saddled and rode his first winner with Flash Parade in the La Touche Memorial Cup at Punchestown.

During a training career that spanned 52 years, Paddy trained innumerable big-race winners both on the flat and over jumps. In 1967, his 7–1 shot Vulpine, ridden by Matt Curran, won the Irish Grand National. Paddy won the National again 12 months later with Herring Gull, who also won the 1968 Tote Novices' Steeplechase to give Paddy his first Cheltenham victory. He won his third Irish National with Dim Wit in 1972 and his fourth with Luska in 1981.

In October 1973, *The Times* published Paddy's picture for the first time, a nod to his extraordinary triumph on the flat when Hurry Harriet, a mare of comparatively humble origins, sprang a 33–1 shock to win the £36,000 Champion Stakes at Newmarket. 'That race was the highlight of my career,' says Paddy. 'She beat Allez France, the best filly in Europe.' Paddy's son Tom, then nine years old, was standing beside the telephone watching the race when Hurry Harriet's owner, Dr Malcolm Thorp, rang from Canada to get the result. 'The race was still in progress so I held the phone near the television so that he could listen to the commentary but, with all the shouting, he hardly heard a thing. I can recall explaining to him afterwards how she had won the race.' As *The Times* put it, her victory was a reminder that 'a small stud or stable is every bit as capable of playing a leading role in racing as those massive affluent empires which we tend to hear so much about'.

Grabel is quite probably the most successful horse you've never heard of. Paddy picked her up in Doncaster for £1,000, recalling her grandmother, Slap Up, a promising flat racer whom he had trained for the Vigors family. Grabel won 26 races for Doninga but none more profitable than the first-ever Dueling Grounds International Hurdle, which took place at Kentucky Downs in 1990. It was the richest steeplechase ever run in North America and Grabel scooped the $750,000 prize. The horse was trained by Paddy, owned by Maureen (and E.F. Keogh) and ridden by their son Tony. T'was a lively night for the Mullins clan down Kentucky way.

Meanwhile, Paddy's success at National Hunt level continued when Sean Treacy of Borris rode the first of many wins for Doninga, taking Nagrada past the post in the Galway Hurdle, a victory made all the sweeter for the fact that the winning owner was Paddy's brother, Captain Luke Mullins, Clerk of the Course at Galway. 'I loved Galway,' says Paddy, 'and I suspect Galway loved me. It was a very lucky track for me, and I never had any major misfortune there. I wouldn't miss going down there for diamonds.'

In 1977, Counsel Cottage survived a shaky final jump to win the Sun Alliance Novices' Hurdle by three lengths and give Paddy his second Cheltenham win. The Master of Doninga also won the National Hunt Chase twice – with Hazy Dawn in 1982 and with Macks Friendly in 1984, both times with son Willie in the saddle.

Paddy is a man who has studiously avoided the limelight, preferring to let his charges feel the heat of the camera flashes. He officially retired in 2005 at the age of 86, handing the yard over to his son Tom. He remained on top of his game to the very end, often mounting an Aidan O'Brien-style multiple-entry challenge on the feature races, a method which frequently proved worthwhile.

In 2003, the octogenarian secured his first Classic success with 12–1 shot Vintage Tipple, under Frankie Dettori, in the Irish Oaks. Her victory was particularly electrifying given that Paddy restored her to health after she had sustained a hairline fracture of her cannon bone.

One of the most remarkable things about the Mullins family is that they have all ridden racecourse winners. Paddy and his four sons were well known on the track. His daughter Sandra McCarthy also won several races, including the Rose of Tralee ladies' race in Tralee. But arguably the most stylish of them all was Paddy's wife Maureen, who, on her first and only contest, rode to victory in a charity race at Gowran Park seated upon a white stallion called Razzo Forte.

HRH Princess Anne and Paddy Mullins at the unveiling of a statue of
Dawn Run at Cheltenham, St Patrick's Day 1987.
(Photographer unknown)

WILLIE MULLINS

Horse Racing

TITLES
Champion Trainer (Ireland), 2008 (110 wins), 2009 (136 wins), 2010 (146 wins)
Champion Amateur Irish Jockey: 6

MAJOR RACE WINS AS TRAINER
Aintree
Martell Grand National: 1

Auteuil
French Champion Hurdle (Grande Course de Haies): 2

Cheltenham
Champion Bumper: 6
Novices' Chase: 3
Supreme Novices' Hurdle: 2
David Nicholson Mares' Hurdle: 2
Sun Alliance Novices' Hurdle: 2
Triumph Hurdle: 1
County Hurdle: 1

Down Royal
Ulster Derby: 2
Champion Chase: 1

Fairyhouse
Bisquit Cognac Handicap Hurdle: 2
Royal Bond Novice Hurdle: 2
Irish Independent Chase: 1
Champion Four-Year-Old Hurdle: 1

Galway
Galway Hurdle: 1

Gowran Park
Thyestes Chase: 3

Kempton Park
King George VI Chase: 1

Leopardstown
Hennessy Gold Cup: 6
Arkle Novice Chase: 3
Dr P.J. Moriarty Novice Chase: 4
MCR Hurdle: 1
Deloitte Novice Hurdle: 1

Listowel
Kerry National: 2

Punchestown
Champion Hurdle: 2
Champion Four-Year-Old Hurdle: 2
Champion Chase: 2
World Series Hurdle: 3
Champion Novice Hurdle (five year olds plus): 2
Champion Novice Hurdle (four year olds plus): 5
Punchestown Gold Cup: 1
Champion Novice Chase: 1

As the 2010 Punchestown Festival began, much of the banter centred upon Willie Mullins and his yard at Closutton, Bagenalstown, Co. Carlow. The question was how on earth could Willie ever hope to better the 2009 Festival, when his team returned home with an unprecedented haul of twelve victories, including four Grade 1 wins. Put another way, a Willie Mullins horse had won almost one in every three races over the course of the week. With his star rider Ruby Walsh out of action as the 2010 Festival commenced, the non-believers were out in force. And then, on the first day, the Mullins yard scored a Grade 1 treble. As anticipation turned to astonishment, Willie duly scored another grand tally of twelve wins, upping his number of Grade 1s to five. He had the first and second in the Champion Novices' Hurdle on Tuesday, the first and third in the Champion Novices' Chase on Wednesday, the first and third in the World Series Hurdle on Thursday and the first and third again in the Champion Hurdle on Friday. It was a truly sensational week.

As with his three younger brothers and sister Sandra, Willie grew up with the scent of the horse all around. At the time of his birth in 1956, Willie's father Paddy Mullins was already on the road that would make him one of the most successful National Hunt trainers of his generation. Young Willie was in the saddle from the age he could toddle. In his boyhood years, he read up as much as he could about the industry, particularly focusing on the methods and problem-solving tactics of other trainers. He continues to be a voracious reader on the subject, always eager to absorb new information and insights into this ancient but ever-evolving sport.

Willie was educated by the Cistercians at Roscrea College, Co. Tipperary. In 1974, he completed his Leaving Certificate and went home to work with his father at Doninga. That same year, he rode his first race as an amateur. He went on to be Irish champion amateur jockey six times.

His Cheltenham career got off to a mighty start on St Patrick's Day 1982, when he had his first ride on English soil upon Hazy Dawn, trained by his father and owned by country-and-western singer Roly Daniels. The race was the four-mile National Hunt Chase at Cheltenham and the mare romped home an impressive winner. Two years later, Willie won the National Hunt Chase again, this time on Macks Friendly. And in between those two victories, he scored the Liverpool Fox Hunters' Chase (the amateurs' Grand National) on Átha Cliath in what was the first all-Irish combination of horse, owner, trainer and rider to win the race.

In 1988, having worked as assistant to both his father and Jim Bolger, Willie took out his own licence for his stables at Bagenalstown on the Carlow–Kilkenny border. He swiftly established himself as a specialist in the Cheltenham Festival Bumper, winning the race a record-breaking six times, thrice in consecutive years. In the 1996 Bumper, 40-year-old Willie was himself in the saddle of the victorious Wither or Which.

Amongst those other bumper heroes was Florida Pearl, one of the greatest of Closutton's flag-bearers. The popular bay beat Best Mate to win the 2001 King George VI Chase, and came second and third in the Cheltenham Gold Cup. But Leopardstown was his preferred ground. He won the Irish Hennessy Gold Cup three years in a row from 1999 to 2001, so becoming the only horse in existence to win a Gold Cup in both the second and third millennium. In 2004, he went on to win the Hennessy for a record fourth time, becoming, at 12 years old, the oldest horse yet to win it. The victory was made all the more poignant by the fact that this was Florida Pearl's final race.

Another of Willie's greatest steeds has been Hedgehunter, whom Ruby Walsh rode to a famous victory in the 2005 Aintree Grand National. In 2006, the Dublin-bred gelding proved to be a most gallant runner-up in the Aintree Grand National, the Cheltenham Gold Cup (to War of Attrition, under Conor O'Dwyer) and the Hennessy Cognac Gold Cup at Leopardstown.

Willie now has 17 Cheltenham wins under his belt. And like his father, he has also enjoyed success both in France, where he has won the Champion Hurdle at Auteuil twice, and on the flat, most notably winning the Ulster Derby twice, with General Cloney in 1999 and with Temlett in 2007.

But it is the National Hunt in Ireland that Willie has completely dominated for the past four years. His tally of 79 winners at the end of 2006–07 was his highest ever and was nearly enough to take Noel Meade's crown as the leading trainer in Ireland. The following season, he secured the crown with 110 wins. At the end of the 2009–10 season, he had racked up an incredible haul of 146 wins, more than 87 higher than his nearest rival, and with earnings of €2.9 million, bringing in more prize money than his nearest three rivals combined. Amongst his strongest performers at present are Quevega, Cooldine and Hurricane Fly.

Willie is very much a twenty-first-century trainer. He's a regular on Twitter and Facebook, and his website is bang up to speed. With more than 100 horses in his charge, he is also well aware of the necessity of having a strong team. His wife, Jackie, herself a champion lady amateur in times past, plays an integral part in the running of the yard and its administration. His top stable jockey is Ruby Walsh, whom he shares with Paul Nicholls, the leading trainer in the UK, but he has plenty more up his sleeve, including his son, three-time champion amateur jockey Patrick Mullins, his nephew Emmet Mullins, David Casey, David Condon, 2010 Punchestown hero Paul Townend and 2010 Cheltenham heroine Miss Katie Walsh.

Willie Mullins gallops the Paddy Mullins-trained Átha Cliath to victory in the 1983 Fox Hunters' Chase at Aintree. (Photographer unknown)

CHARLIE SWAN

Horse Racing

Wins (as jockey): 1,314
Cheltenham wins: 17

NOTABLE RIDES
Istabraq (Cheltenham Champion Hurdle, 1998, 1999, 2000)
Danoli (Royal & Sun Alliance Novices' Hurdle, 1994)
Viking Flagship (Queen Mother Champion Chase, 1995)
Ebony Jane (Irish Grand National, 1993)
Usher's Island (Whitbread Gold Cup, 1994)
Life of a Lord (Whitbread Gold Cup, 1996)

Culloden, 1746. More than a thousand Scotsmen lie dead. The Duke of Cumberland's victorious English troops are running rampant in the Highlands. One of the duke's most trusted officers lies unconscious, presumed dead. A rattle of prison keys. A young Jacobite surgeon is pulled from his cell and taken to the seemingly lifeless man. The doctor sets to work. A spluttering, blood-soaked cough and the officer awakens. He will survive. 'A life for a life,' barks the duke, with one eye on the Scottish surgeon. He is to be pardoned but must leave Scotland. The duke goes on to co-found the English Jockey Club and breed a horse called Eclipse, the greatest sire of the eighteenth century. And the surgeon, whose name was Swan, moves to Lincolnshire and becomes the ancestral sire of Charlie Swan, one of the finest jump jockeys of the late twentieth century.

'Did my father tell you all that?' marvels Charlie, the horse beneath him turning full circle. 'It gets better every time.'

Horse and jockey clatter off up the gallops, kicking dust into the sky. Straight ahead are the Slieve Bloom Mountains. But otherwise this north-western corner of Co. Tipperary is a horizontal landscape. As local patriot Thomas MacDonagh wrote, it is a place 'in calm of middle country'.

Captain Donald Swan, Charlie's father, moved here from England in the 1960s. A former dragoon, he was also a passionate huntsman. 'I rode in the Grand National,' he says proudly, and then mutters, 'Didn't get very far.' He had more success at Sandown, notching up a few winners. His regiment was later posted to Ulster. 'I used to do a lot of race riding in the south, steeplechasing and point-to-points, in a fun amateur way, and I fell in love with Ireland.'

In time, Donald inherited some money and purchased Modreeny House, near Cloughjordan, with 200 acres. 'The house hadn't been lived in for 15 years,' he says. 'There were chickens upstairs and sheep downstairs. It was just being used as a barn.' Adjacent to the house lay the ruins of an O'Carroll castle, destroyed by Cromwell's troops as they marched from Birr to Limerick. Legend holds that the O'Carroll treasure lies submerged beneath the land; ambitious descendants occasionally appear with metal detectors.

From Modreeny, Donald hunted the Ormond Hunt for a while and later the Golden Vale. While he primarily farmed, he also began training a half-dozen racehorses. And when his small son Charlie began to clamber into the saddle, Donald realised he was the father of a very talented boy.

Both Charlie and Donald agree that the 'jockey genes' come from his mother. Teresa's grandfather, Tom Chaloner, was champion jockey in 1863, when he won both the 2,000 Guineas and the Derby on Macaroni.

Charlie was born in the house in January 1968 with the aid of a local midwife. He was educated at Headfort School, Kells, Co. Meath, and Wilson's Hospital, Multyfarnham, Co. Westmeath. He first tasted victory aged 12 at a pony race in Ballinasloe. Three years later, he had his first win on the flat at Naas, riding Final Assault, bred by his father and owned by his grandmother Nina Swan. 'It really was a wonderful family win,' says Donald.

Charlie put the pressure on his parents to let him leave school early so that he could focus on being a jockey. He was apprenticed to Kevin Prendergast at the Curragh, and also won a 1,000 guineas trial on John Hayden's The Banshee.

With his weight rising, he transferred to jumps. His first break came when Paddy Mullins gave him the ride of Ash Creek, which won the 1984 Hennessy Handicap at Leopardstown. By the time he moved to Dessie Hughes' yard at the age of 16, Charlie's phenomenal career was well under way.

Over the next 19 years, he rode 1,314 winners, including 17 at Cheltenham, where he was leading jockey in both 1993 and 1994. He was nine-time champion jockey in Ireland and, before Ruby Walsh arrived on the scene, had won more races over jumps in Ireland than any other jockey.

'I never stopped trying to improve as a rider,' he says. 'You should never think that you have conquered everything.'

His bugbear was the Aintree Grand National. 'I always had a fixation on it,' he says. 'When I was a kid I taped every race and I'd watch them over and over again.' However, while he can reel off the names of every winner since Rubstic in 1979, the best he could manage was second place in the 1993 Aintree Grand National, the one that was declared void due to a false start. Charlie went on to win the Irish Grand National on the mare Ebony Jane nine days later.

J.P. McManus, one of Charlie's most devoted followers, once described him as 'a master technician and the most knowledgeable jockey I have ever spoken to'. J.P. was owner of the horse with which Charlie will forever be associated, namely Istabraq. A portrait of this handsome bay holds pride of place in Charlie's kitchen. Istabraq was arguably the best two-mile hurdler of modern times, winning the Champion Hurdle three years in a row. Charlie rode Istabraq in all 29 of his races over jumps, bringing in more than a million pounds sterling in prize money. Every now and then he goes to visit Istabraq, who is now munching merrily on J.P.'s meadows. 'He's in great order,' says Charlie. 'He gets looked after like a king.'

Statisticians reckon a jockey falls off his horse every four races, so it should come as no surprise that Charlie was on first-name terms with hospital staff across Britain and Ireland. He has no idea how many times he fell but 'it must be well over a hundred'. His father has a chart showing his miscellaneous injuries. Broken nose, lost front teeth, fractured skull, broken collarbone, fractured ribs, broken leg, broken foot, broken wrist, broken hand, cracked little finger, punctured lung, three breaks to left arm, three breaks to right arm, scarred lip, broken vertebrae, facial scarring over eye and on forehead. 'People say how lucky he was,' muses Donald, 'but he's had his fair share of break-ups.'

At the age of 35, Charlie rode his last race on board Like-A-Butterfly in the 2003 Aintree meeting. 'It was a natural progression to hang up my boots and go training. I always said I'd stop at 35. After the high of Istabraq, I didn't want to go out on a low, riding the odd time on hard ground and summer tracks . . .'

'You lost your nerve basically,' teases his wife who, as Carol Hyde, was no slouch in the saddle; she was frequently to be seen flying over fences six foot high and won fourteen races herself. Her jockey grandfather Timmy Hyde won the Aintree and Irish Grand Nationals, as well as the Cheltenham Gold Cup.

As a retirement present, J.P. McManus presented Charlie with a *This Is Your Life*-style book called *Swansong*, charting his career from Ballinasloe onwards. A new chapter began as Charlie saddled his first winner as a full-time trainer when Fawn Prince scored at Bellewstown. He has learned a lot by simply observing while based at yards of trainers like Dessie Hughes, Aidan O'Brien and Martin Pipe. He now has more than 65 horses in training and has trained more than 400 winners, including One Cool Cookie, winner of the 2007 Powers Gold Cup at Fairyhouse.

'Riding was definitely easier,' he says. 'When you're training you can't just walk away after a race. You have to deal with owners and their disappointments. It is a tough job, and not everybody would have the temperament for it. If you were in any way uptight or nervous, you'd never be able to relax.'

Charlie Swan rode the last of his 17 Cheltenham winners in 2002, when he galloped the Willie Mullins-trained Scolardy home in the JCB Triumph Hurdle.
(© Damien Eagers/Sportsfile)

RUBY WALSH

Horse Racing

Wins: *c.*1,800
Cheltenham wins: 25

TITLES
Cheltenham Champion Jockey: 5
British Horseracing Board Jockeys' Order of Merit Award, 2007

NOTABLE RIDES
Kauto Star (Cheltenham Gold Cup, 2007, 2009; King George VI Chase, 2006, 2007, 2008, 2009)
Papillon (Aintree Grand National, 2000)
Hedgehunter (Aintree Grand National, 2005)
Azertyuiop (Queen Mother Champion Chase, 2004)
Master Minded (Queen Mother Champion Chase, 2008, 2009)
Commanche Court (Irish Grand National, 2000)
Numbersixvalverde (Irish Grand National, 2005)
Silver Birch (Welsh Grand National, 2004)
Take Control (Scottish Grand National, 2002)
Strong Flow (Hennessy Gold Cup, 2003)
Denman (Hennessy Gold Cup, 2009)

There's a modest crowd out for the Thurles races. It's cloudy, the ground is soft and the bookies are chattering easily with one another as they slowly hoist the odds for the opening race. The jockeys have been ambling into their changing-rooms slowly, some in gabbling pairs, some sullen and heads low.

We didn't see Ruby enter. He must have slipped in through a door at the back. An elderly couple are standing close by, craning their necks excitedly every time the door to the jockeys' enclosure creaks open. 'We're waiting on Ruby,' says the lady in Australian. 'We've followed him all the way from Cheltenham.' Her eyes sparkle with giddy anticipation, a hint, perhaps, of a schoolgirl who once chased The Beatles down streets with her mouth at full scream. 'You see, horses don't jump in Australia . . .' begins

her husband. And then Ruby strolled out the door. 'Ruby, Ruby, Ruby,' whispers the Australian lady.

The five-time champion jockey was calm but running a little late. It was 2.25 p.m. and in 20 minutes he was due to ride a horse called Black Harry for Willie Mullins at the meeting's opener. He paused for long enough to stand with the Australians while the camera clicked. Far from screaming, the lady was so star-struck that she didn't say a word. Ruby was ours for seven minutes and three seconds. We walked and talked. James sat him in the stand and took his photo.

It had been a busy month for the most successful National Hunt jockey in Irish history. Six days earlier, he had been crowned 'King of Cheltenham' when he notched up his 25th win, more than anyone else in the 108 years since the festival began. At the 2009 Festival, he had ridden a record-breaking seven Cheltenham winners over the four days, which placed him in pole position to seize the crown in 2010. But Ruby would be first to admit that for a while it looked like he might not have even been top jockey in his own household during the Cheltenham week, as his younger sister Katie galloped home with two wins.

Rupert Walsh was born in Naas on 14 May 1979. His father, Ted, was Ireland's leading amateur jockey eleven times, and won four races at Cheltenham. He is a racehorse trainer with an Aintree Grand National under his belt. Ted is also one of RTÉ's foremost racing presenters, well known for his frank and well-informed humour. And judging by Ruby's own acclaimed performance as his father's deputy during the coverage of Punchestown 2010, the younger Walsh can certainly consider a future as a television pundit.

Ruby's quietly spoken grandfather and namesake Ruby Walsh Sr ran a pub with a livery stable in Fermoy, Co. Cork. During the 1950s, the Walsh family spent two years in the USA, where Ruby senior's brother Micky trained jumpers. Ruby senior obtained his training licence in 1956 and rented stables in Chapelizod. He later moved to Kill, close to the Goffs sales arena in Co. Kildare, and began operating as a small-time trainer with 12 stables. Ted and his wife Helen, daughter of a garda sergeant, moved to Kill in 1984, where they raised their four children on the small farm which now runs to sixty acres. Ruby senior passed away on New Year's Day 1991. 'I knew him well,' says his grandson. 'He was a lovely man.'

Ruby was a boy of many sports, a Man United fan and a gifted scrum-half who once got an Under-16s trial with the Leinster rugby team. But the world of the gee-gees was ingrained deep within him. As a schoolboy he rode out for Enda Bolger, the cross-country specialist trainer. He was 16 years old and a 7 lb-claiming amateur when he first met Willie Mullins. In November 1995, Willie was due to ride an awkward filly called Young Fenora at Leopardstown. He took a punt and offered the ride to Ruby, who duly sailed home to victory. 'I wouldn't know a hurler or a footballer if they hit me in the face,' said Willie. 'But I know a jockey and I just thought to myself, that's not ordinary stuff.'

When the 1996–97 season ended, 18-year-old Ruby was Ireland's top amateur jockey. He won the title again the following season and turned professional. In 1998, he opened his account at the Cheltenham Festival with a win on Alexander Banquet in the Champion Bumper.

The first year of the millennium was to be an astonishing one for the Walshes. Ruby rode the bay Papillon, trained by his father, to win the Aintree Grand National, the holy grail of the National Hunt. It was Ruby's first crack at the race but, as he says, it's not

always good for the nerves to know what the jump ahead is going to be like.

Sixteen days later, father and son won the Irish National at Fairyhouse with Commanche Court. Ruby thus became the first jockey to complete the Irish–English National double since Tommy Carberry nearly thirty years earlier.

In 2004–05, Ruby scored an extraordinary hat-trick, winning the English, Irish and Welsh Grand Nationals. He also nearly won the Scottish National, but was beaten by a short head. Nonetheless, the fact that he had previously won the Scottish National in 2002 makes him the only jockey currently riding to have won all four Grand Nationals.

Ruby's brilliance stems from his ability to create a vital synergy between himself and the horses beneath him. He understands how to read their temperament and he has the power to keep that chemistry going through to the final sprint to the line. 'The horse has to go along with you,' he says. 'If he doesn't, you'll win no race.'

In just over 10 years, the Kildare man has won more than 1,800 races, including his 25 wins at the Cheltenham Festival. As well as his five Cheltenham champion jockey crowns, he has won the Irish jump jockey title seven times since his professional debut in 1998. So exceptional a jockey is he that he is even the subject of a song, Christy Moore's charming 'Ballad of Ruby Walsh'.

His command of the sport is such that he is able to persuade Willie Mullins and Paul Nicholls, the champion trainers of Ireland and England respectively, to share him as their

On 7 April 2010, Ruby Walsh rode Askmeroe to victory in the Broad Meadow Beginners' Steeplechase at the Fairyhouse Festival. Three days later, Ireland's champion jockey broke his arm at Aintree and was out for the rest of the season. (© Brian Lawless/Sportsfile)

stable jockey. He has been blessed with many extraordinary mounts, most memorably the Nicholls-trained Kauto Star, with whom Ruby has won two Cheltenham Gold Cups and four King George VI Chases.

National Hunt racing is surely the only sport in which an ambulance pursues the performers as they race. Ruby has lost count of the number of times he has been catapulted from the saddle and crashed to the ground. I am given a short topographical tour of his body as he pinpoints the injuries that helped turn his hair grey – dislocations, breaks, fractures, crushes, severances. He once returned to racing 28 days after his spleen was removed. 'There's no stopping,' he says, his dark, mischievous eyes looking briefly exhausted. 'Save maybe ten days in June.'

And then he was off. Black Harry came third, which would have been fine if it hadn't been a five-horse race.

As for Ruby, he broke his left arm in the race before his friend Tony McCoy won the 2010 Aintree Grand National. At least that gave him a few months off to contemplate life as a TV pundit and kick back with his wife Gillian and baby daughter Isabelle at their home in Calverstown, Co. Kildare. In July 2010, he was also able to lend a helping, albeit fractured, hand as caddy to McCoy for the J.P. McManus pro-am charity golf tournament in Adare.

CONOR O'DWYER

Horse Racing

Wins (as jockey): *c.*700
Cheltenham wins: 4

NOTABLE RIDES
Imperial Call (Cheltenham Gold Cup, 1996; Hennessy Gold Cup, 1996)
War of Attrition (Cheltenham Gold Cup, 2006)
Hardy Eustace (Cheltenham Champion Hurdle, 2004, 2005; AIG Champion Hurdle, 2007)
Native Upmanship (Powers Gold Cup, 2000; Martell Melling Chase, 2002, 2003)
Mister Top Notch (Pierse Leopardstown Handicap Chase, 2008)

As she passed him the Gold Cup, the Queen Mother caught Conor O'Dwyer's eye and whispered, 'I'm sorry it's not full.' The jockey from Co. Wexford chuckled hard. This was a moment to savour. It was 14 March 1996 and he had just ridden Imperial Call to victory in Ireland's first success at the Cheltenham Gold Cup since Dawn Run a decade earlier. The crowd were so ecstatic that, as he was bounced from shoulder to shoulder, the 29-year-old jockey wondered whether his saddle and lead weights might already have been nabbed as souvenirs.

Winning the Gold Cup is every jockey's dream. Conor did it twice. His victory on Imperial Call was a staggering performance. 'Conor rode a copybook race,' said the gelding's Cork-based trainer, Fergie Sutherland. 'He kept him wide, got him jumping, kicked on and then let the horse's class do the rest.'

Ten years later, Conor made St Patrick's Day his own when he won the 2006 Gold Cup on the Michael O'Leary-owned War of Attrition.

In between the two Gold Cups, Conor racked up a huge tally of victories, most notably back-to-back wins of the Cheltenham Champion Hurdle on Co. Carlow's hugely popular Hardy Eustace.

Such a winning streak was undoubtedly inspired by the fact Conor has a special disposition which horses can relate to. It is also a lot to do with several decades of hard graft.

It was certainly not in the blood. In fact, Conor cannot find any ancestral links to horses at all. The closest he can manage is that his paternal grandfather, John O'Dwyer, was a carpenter based in Enniscorthy, Co. Wexford, who once constructed some confessional boxes for the Catholic Church on the Curragh, where Conor now trains.

Senan O'Dwyer, Conor's late father, enjoyed a few years of oceanic cruising as a radio officer in the Merchant Navy. During a stopover in Liverpool, he met a nurse by name of Kay Gaul, who was working in the city's Walton Street Hospital. Her father, Alderman James Gaul, had served as Mayor of Wexford in 1952. The couple married and returned to Wexford Town, where Senan set himself up as an accountant for an American firm and Kay went to work at Wexford General Hospital, of which she would later become matron.

In the eighteenth century, prospective admirals joined the navy at the age of 12 so they would have a decade of experience under their belt by the time they reached adulthood. The equestrian world trots a similar path and many of the young men and women who gallop past the posts of Cheltenham, Aintree, Leopardstown and Punchestown have been clambering into saddles since they were fetlock high to a grasshopper.

'I started riding when I was six,' says Conor. 'After school I often went to see a good friend of mine called John Berry, whose family are steeped in horses. We'd head out and ride ponies.' He soon persuaded his parents to buy him a pony of his own. 'By the time I was nine, I had made up my mind to be a jockey and I stuck with it and thank God it paid me well enough.'

When he was 14, his parents enrolled him at the newly established Racing Apprentice Centre of Education on the Curragh.

'RACE is really a fantastic facility,' says Conor. 'It used to be that if you made it, you made it, and if you didn't, tough. Next thing your jockey dreams are up in smoke and you're a stable boy. But now they really guide you along so, for example, if you look like you're going to be too big to be an amateur, they will advise you what job to go for.'

Jockeys are made of sturdy stuff. They don't need to do push-ups or run miles or swim a hundred lengths to stay fit. They simply get up on a horse and ride out. Conor was soon riding out eight horses every morning. His talent, determination and light frame caught the eye of local trainers who began to offer him race rides.

'Riding out is great but there's nothing like the actual racecourse rides,' he says. 'A good rider at home doesn't always make it on the track. You need to race as often as you can so you can feel it all, and if you've messed up, then you watch the race again on TV and see where you went wrong. You've got to be very, very self-critical. If you don't find fault, you won't prove anything.'

He completed the pre-apprentice jockey course in 1982 and rode his first race in Roscommon shortly afterwards. Two years and eight races later, the sixteen year old rode his first winner in a claiming bumper at Limerick.

Progress was slow in the early years but he secured his first major victory in the 1991 Ladbroke Handicap Hurdle at Leopardstown on board the Paddy Mullins-trained Redundant Pal. Five years later, he became a household name with his sensational Gold Cup victory on Imperial Call. 'It's everybody's dream to win at Cheltenham,' he says. 'The dream of every jockey, owner and trainer. Cheltenham is the Olympics of racing so to win the Gold Cup was incredible.

'Ninety per cent of my career has been luck,' he says. 'Being in the right place at the right time.' One of his most fortuitous decisions was to turn down an offer to become stable jockey to Kim Bailey in England and take up with Arthur Moore in Co. Kildare instead. 'I didn't want to leave home,' he explains. He enjoyed a very successful ten years with Mr Moore, most notably partnering Native Upmanship to twelve victories between 1999 and 2005.

'In my best years, I rode between 400 and 500 different horses a year,' Conor reckons. By the time he retired, after 26 seasons, he had racked up more than 700 wins. He rode his last race on Easter Monday 2008, steering Mr Top Notch to victory in the Pierse Leopardstown Handicap Chase. 'I had mixed emotions about retiring but I thought I'd get out on a good note. Racing is a young man's sport and you have to be hungry and fit and determined. I'd started training and both jobs require 100 per cent. Something had to go.'

His one regret is that he never won the Grand National. 'I was third in it the first year I rode and I had another 14 goes after that. It's not necessarily the classiest race but I still wanted to win it.'

Perhaps he might win it as a trainer. He began his new career in 2008 and trains amid the white railings of the Curragh's gallops, a landscape he has known intimately since he was 14.

Recession aside, he is 'very happy with the way things are going', notching up the first win of his new career when Hangover won a bumper at Punchestown in 2008. In June 2010, Conor trained D for Dave, the horse that pulled off an extraordinary betting coup when it won the Hurley Family Handicap Hurdle at Kilbeggan just five minutes after its owner gave 200 runners €200 each to place on the seven-length winner.

He believes the racing industry has been revolutionised in the past decade and that everything has become steadily more serious and competitive. It is his hope that he can inject a fresh and positive spark, that one of his horses might emerge as the new Moscow Flyer or Hardy Eustace and draw the cheering crowds.

Conor takes time out every August to return to his native Co. Wexford, where his family have a summer house in Kilmore Quay. His preferred place of sanctuary is on board a small fishing boat, swishing around the Saltee Islands and Tuskar Rock.

Conor O'Dwyer and Hardy Eustace victoriously acknowledge the crowd after their second consecutive victory in the Smurfit Champion Hurdle at Cheltenham in 2005.
(© Brendan Moran/Sportsfile)

EDDIE MACKEN

Showjumping

ACHIEVEMENTS
Olympic Games: 1992, 1996, 2004 (as team trainer)
World Championships: 1974 (silver), 1978 (silver), 1982, 1990, 1994
European Championships: 1973, 1977 (silver), 1978 (silver), 1979, 1981, 1983, 1995, 1997
World Cup: 1979, 1984, 1986, 1992, 1994, 1995, 1996
Hickstead Derby: 1976, 1977, 1978, 1979
Dublin Nations Cup (Aga Khan Trophy): 1977, 1978, 1979, 1984, 1987, 1990, 1992, 1995, 1997

AWARDS
Texaco Special Achievement Award, 1976, 1978
Texaco Sportstars Award, 1974, 1976, 1977, 1978, 1979

In 1935, the late folklorist James G. Delaney interviewed an elderly butcher from Granard, Co. Longford, about the Irish Famine. The butcher, whose name was Bernard Macken, recounted a story told about his grandfather, who had a farm at Granardkill at this time. The year was 1847 and death from famine was widespread across Co. Longford. As the funeral bell from the nearby chapel resounded yet again across the fields, Bernard's grandfather exhaled.

'God bless us, how many times have I heard that bell today!' he said.

'Now is the time to bury them – when the ground is soft,' replied one of the men who worked on the farm.

'My grandfather was so angry at the fellow's callous remark,' said Bernard, 'that he ran him and would not employ him. The next week the workman was a-burying himself.'

It is not known when Bernard set up his butcher's shop but it was certainly in operation in 1911, by which time he was married with three sons. Seventy years later, Bernard's grandson Eddie Macken, unarguably the greatest showjumping superstar that Ireland has produced, would attribute his sense of balance to a childhood spent 'carrying sides of beef' in the family shop.

Eddie's father Jimmy, who inherited the business, likewise recalled how his son taught himself to ride using 'the stools in my butcher shop, the chairs at home, the walls and whatever he could find . . . and even then he rode them with style'.

'My only dream was to ride horses,' says Eddie. 'It's the closest thing to flying.' From butcher's stools he graduated to farm ponies and neighbours' horses. Older people still

remember the time he came clattering through Granard's main street on a pony, dressed in his new Christmas cowboy gear, blasting his toy six-shooter into the sky.

In 1961, Eddie's focus sharpened when his hero Séamus Hayes won the first-ever Hickstead Derby in England. Eddie was a pupil at St Mel's College in Granard at this time. The instant school was finished he would run down to the local equestrian centre, run by vet Brian Gormley and his wife Ann, to take their ponies out for a spin and hone his technique.

In 1969, the 'rough country boy' caught the eye of legendary trainer Iris Kellett. 'He had an excellent build, was supple, had the temperament and natural sensitivity,' she recalled. 'Above everything else he had a feel for the horse.'

Miss Kellett took Eddie on as a working student at her stables on the Mespil Road in Dublin. When she retired from international showjumping in 1972, she passed over her horses to him, including the great Morning Light.

Within eight months, Eddie was on Ireland's Aga Khan Trophy team. Astonishingly he was still on the Irish team 36 years later, and during those long decades no showjumper had ever done more to bring Ireland to its feet.

Eddie's most famous partnership was with Boomerang, a Tipperary-bred gelding that stood 16.2 hands high. Their union was straight off the pages of a Jilly Cooper novel. Boomerang had once been in Miss Kellett's yard but Eddie found him difficult to ride and the horse was sold onwards.

In August 2008, Eddie Macken returned to the Dublin Horse Show, riding Tedechine Sept in the Aga Khan Nations Cup. Thirty-six years had passed since he first rode out for Ireland in the contest, during which time the Co. Longford man had established himself as one of the world's greatest showjumping legends. (© Brian Lawless/Sportsfile)

In the spring of 1975, Eddie was riding with the wealthy Schockemöhle brothers at Mühlen, West Germany, when his best horse, Easter Parade, unexpectedly broke its back. Amongst the horses in Paul Schockemöhle's yard was an Irish horse owned by the German oil magnate Dr Herbert Schnapka. 'Take this horse until you get something better,' suggested Paul. That horse was Boomerang and, in due course, Dr Schnapka gifted him to Eddie.

Together with his first wife Susanne, Eddie patiently and intuitively trained Boomerang with such success that whenever he hopped into the saddle, something quite magical happened. Showjumping horses are not generally household names but by the time Boomerang was retired with a fractured pedal bone in the summer of 1980, there was hardly a soul in Ireland who did not know his name.

Between 1975 and 1979, the pair won, or took second, in a record-breaking 32 major Grand Prix or Derby events across Europe and the USA, from Dublin to Rome to Madison Square Garden. They also won a record £250,000 in prize money.

When the redoubtable stallion was put down three years later, he was buried in a field at Rafeehan, the Mackens' stud near Kells, Co. Meath. Four evergreens were planted around his grave, symbolising Eddie and Boomerang's record of four consecutive Hickstead Derby wins (still unparalleled), four Wembley championships, four clear rounds in the 1978 World Championship final, and four years in a row without knocking a fence at the Aga Khan Trophy in Dublin.

The Dublin Horse Show has rarely been as thrilling as it was in those years when he captained James Kernan, Paul Darragh and Con Power to win three Aga Khans in a row and give Ireland its greatest showjumping revival since the 1930s. Hailed as 'the supreme stylist', Eddie was also an extremely consistent, bankable and electrifying performer. In an age when Ireland was in dire need of heroes, he grabbed every title on offer, often scooping second place on a different horse in the same event. He topped the World Commuter Ratings in 1976, 1977 and 1978.

By 1980, both Boomerang and Kerrygold, Eddie's other outstanding steed, had been retired. At that year's Dublin Horse Show, Eddie piloted the chestnut gelding Carroll's Royal Lion to win the Puissance on a bucketing wet August afternoon. The roars of delight that emanated from beneath the multicoloured umbrellas of those who watched him win sashayed all the way around Ballsbridge, rippling through Miss Bay Jellett's Orchestra and harmonising with the drum beats of the Army Band of the Southern Command.

Eddie's later career was not without controversy. On the opening morning of the 1985 Dublin Horse Show, he joined Paul Darragh and Paul Duffy on a strike in protest against a rule which imposed an army chef d'équipe (team leader) whenever there were two or more army men on the Irish team. Intense negotiations ensued and the three men ultimately rejoined the squad, but the event was evidence that the golden age of Irish showjumping had come to an end.

By 1996, Eddie had relocated to Germany, where he rode for millionaire industrialist Michael Nixdorf. Earlier this century, he moved to Langley, east of Vancouver, where he set up the New Kells Farm with his present wife Kathi Ballentine. He still competed for Ireland and in 1998 he took part in his 27th consecutive Aga Khan.

In 2004, Eddie was appointed chef de mission to the Irish team for the Athens Olympics. When Eddie was ingloriously dismissed, the riders refused to continue until he was reinstated. He was duly restored, working alongside Ned Campion, but the team's subsequent success was overshadowed by the loss of Cian O'Connor's Olympic gold after his horse Waterford Crystal tested positive in a doping test.

In July 2008, the 59 year old returned to Hickstead for the first time in a decade. The following month, the crowds gathered in the sun-drenched Anglesea Stand at the RDS roared their approval as Eddie jumped clear in a flawless round to clinch a creditable second place in the Aga Khan. Whether the 61-year-old legend will continue to ride for Ireland in the future remains to be seen but there can be no doubt that his extraordinary drive almost single-handedly popularised showjumping as an Irish sport.

TOMMY BRENNAN

Showjumping and Three-Day Eventing

ACHIEVEMENTS
World Championship, 1966, gold
Olympics, 1964, 4th
Winner of 9 RDS National Championships

AWARDS
Gold Badge of Honour, Fédération Équestre Internationale, 1985
Irish Sports Council Hall of Fame, 1997
Three-Day Event Team of the Millennium, 2000

You've clearly done something right when, nearly 40 years after you won a gold medal for Ireland, you walk into a room to find 600 people gathered to celebrate a 'This Is Your Life' evening all about you. Such was the predicament that legendary Olympic showjumper Tommy Brennan found himself plunged into on the first evening of the 2003 Punchestown Three-Day Event. Whether he knew about the occasion in advance is unclear. He was probably far too busy marching about the cross-country course in his trademark bowler, checking all 23 fences were still in order. But as he heard those 1,200 hands clapping, and listened to the tales from so many he has known, it must have all come flooding back.

Tommy Brennan was born in 1940 on the family farm at Dunnamaggin, Co. Kilkenny. The land rolls along the banks of the King's and Glory rivers, midway between Kells and Kilmoganny. It's a happy landscape, where flowers, blackberries and mushrooms grow wild and beautiful on the sunny slopes of Cloyninnie. Seventeen huge lime trees rise from the earth alongside the old round tower of Kilree.

Loughsullis, the name of the farm, means 'Pond of Brightness' and it had been in the family for many long generations. 'The headstone of my forbears goes Mathew, Thomas, Mathew, Thomas, way back to the 1700s. My grandfather was Thomas and my father was Matty.'

Margaret Brennan, Tommy's mother, was the granddaughter of Richard and Henriette Duggan, who ran a drapery in Kilkenny City. Her father and uncle later converted it into the Monster House, a once iconic department store with five in-house tailors. 'The women

would go around serving customers tea from pots on crochet napkins,' recalls Tommy. 'My grandfather was a horseman and always gave fellow horsemen a 10 per cent discount.'

Undoubtedly the most influential of the 'Big House' families in Co. Kilkenny at this time were the McCalmonts of Mount Juliet. At one stage they hunted three days a week and Tommy, who grew up just four miles away, rode out with them every Saturday. He recalls how house guests were met by a groom, dressed in cap and livery, who would take their horses away to be prepared and saddled for the day's hunting. Everyone would then 'hack hell out of it' for two miles to clear away any cobwebs from the night before and calm their hunters down.

At the age of 14, Tommy enrolled at Macra na Feirme in Kells, Co. Kilkenny, through whom he was trained in animal husbandry. In 1956, he became chairman of the Young Farmers Association.

Tommy decided to further his equestrian and agricultural education by moving to Skidoo Stud in Dublin, owned by Dutch industrialist Omar van Landeghem. 'Omar Van' exported in excess of 50,000 head of cattle a year and Tommy was given a key role in orchestrating the operation. His boss was impressed and soon the young man was running the stud.

During this time, Tommy struck up a famous partnership with a horse called Kilkenny. In 1964, Tommy and Kilkenny flew to Tokyo to compete at the Olympics in the three-day event. They came an admirable fourth. Two years later, the pair rode out for Ireland again at the World Championships at Burghley. The Irish team performed like a dream and won gold. 'That was certainly my career highlight,' says Tommy.

Between 1963 and 1968, Tommy represented Ireland all across the world and won 67 international events. In 1968, he flew out for the Mexican Olympics, where he became the first Irishman – and only the third person in the world – to compete in both showjumping and eventing. Unfortunately, just one month before the games, Tubber Mac, his trusty steed, broke his leg at the water jump in the Dublin Horse Show. 'That was a sad day,' he says. 'Over 20,000 people were watching. It is a long and lonely walk from the RDS arena to the pocket with just your saddle and bridle.'

In 1969, Tommy's father died and he inherited the family's 180-acre farm at Loughsullis, complete with crumbling thatched farmhouse. His subsequent improvements to the farm earned him the 1970 Farmer of the Year Award. He was singled out for the presentation of his 500-strong herd of cattle, sport and thoroughbred horses, as well as the intelligent layout of buildings and facilities, and the management of grasslands and hedges.

His achievements caught the eye of an upcoming politician called Charlie Haughey. In 1969, Mr Haughey invited Tommy to manage his 250-acre stud at Abbeville. Tommy stayed there for eight 'great years', looking after jumpers, racehorses, thoroughbreds and hunters, as well as creating a cross-country course and an indoor school.

Following the death of his younger brother Larry in 1979, Tommy sold Loughsullis. He moved to Co. Meath, where he ran the Loughmore Stud and rode out with the Meath Hunt, the Ward Union and the Fingal Harriers. Amongst the horses he bred was San Scilla, who won the French Guineas. He was also closely associated with nine horses, both jumpers and eventers, who competed at the Olympics.

And then there was Ambassador, another of the mighty steeds with which he will forever be associated. 'We won everything together from Hickstead to Dortmund to Holland,'

Tommy recalls. 'He wasn't all that consistent but he liked the big jumps.' In 1972, Tommy was again selected for the Irish team for the Munich Olympics. However, the Equestrian Federation of Ireland rejected his qualification. Their decision, which still aggravates Tommy 50 years later, was based on the fact that, as he had set up Dublin Bloodstock Ltd, an agency, he was deemed to have turned professional. Tommy took it to court, where, too late, the judge concurred that just because one is a director of Guinness, that does not make one a professional barman. Meanwhile, Ambassador went to Munich and won what remains the only Olympic gold won by an Irish horse. Rubbing salt in the wound, he was ridden by Graziano Mancinelli, the biggest professional rider in the sport. 'The Olympic rules were a sham at that time,' says Tommy.

In the early 1980s, Tommy turned his expertise to management. He was chef d'équipe to the Irish junior team from 1981 to 1985, winning one gold, two silver and a bronze, including silver at the three-day event at the Burghley Inter-EU Championships. He then became chef for the senior team who won the 2007 Nations Cup at Lynx in Austria, Drammen in Norway and Poznań in Poland.

For many, Tommy's name is synonymous with the three-day event at Punchestown. He was responsible for laying out those much-admired cross-country courses, including the famous replicas of the crannógs and Newgrange that greeted the 60,000-strong crowd who watched Ireland win silver at the 1991 European Championships. Few can rival him for creating a challenging course and he has it down to such a fine art that he can

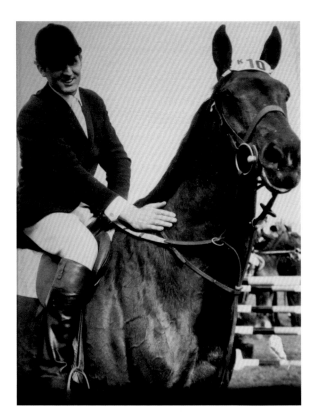

Tommy Brennan on the McDowells' Knorr Swiss, which, as an eight year old, won at both the RDS Dublin Horse Show and the RDS Spring Show in 1968. (Photographer unknown)

practically dictate how many horses will actually succeed in making it around. Safety is paramount. Nearly twenty people have died eventing during the past six years. 'I have been lucky,' says Tommy but nonetheless that figure does not sit easily with him.

As an international course designer, he has made his mark at Punchestown and Tattersalls, as well as Melbourne, Qatar, Estonia and China. In 2003, fellow Irishman Kevin Connolly secured Tommy a lucrative contract from the Beijing Jockey Club to design the 5,000 m cross-country course for the 2008 Equestrian Olympics. Tommy made six trips to the Chinese capital and all was going swimmingly until the BJC and the Chinese government had a fall-out over gambling rights and quarantine. The BJC withdrew their sponsorship, the games were handed over to the Hong Kong Jockey Club and 'my contract was out the window', sighs Tommy.

From Aachen to Zürich, Badminton to Burghley, Tommy won more than a thousand first prizes in twelve years, including a DAF Convertible and a Ford Mustang. In Ireland alone, he has won nine national championships on nine different horses at the Dublin Horse Show and Spring Show. He has tried his hand at everything equestrian from the high jump (2 m 20 cm at Turin, Italy) to the point-to-point (nine wins from twelve starts).

Since 2004, he has been based at Pat and Susan O'Loughlin's Belfield Stud, near Kilpedder, Co. Wicklow, where he is looking after 'a selection of steeplechasers'. 'It's a lovely county, Wicklow, summer or winter,' he says, 'a paradise of tranquillity.' His house is bedecked with memories of the past – photographs of his jumping days, standing with princesses and taoiseachs, Snaffles prints and witty ballads. He remains one of the most popular bachelors in Ireland.

BIBLIOGRAPHY

Allen, Aoife, *Tennis Lives: A Journey Through the Heart of Irish Tennis* (Tennis Ireland, 2008)

Anon, 'Galway for the Races', a souvenir guide to Galway Races (My Parish Publishing, 2006)

Coghlan, Eamonn, with George Kimball, *Chairman of the Boards, Master of the Mile* (Red Rock Press, 2008)

Corcoran, Margaret, 'Profile: Mary Dinan', *Courtside*, Vols 1–2, November/December 1993 (Leinster & Irish Branch of Badminton Union of Ireland)

Delany, Ronnie, *Staying the Distance* (O'Brien Press, 2006)

Harrington, Jessie, *Moscow Flyer: Flying to Success* (Highdown, 2005)

Holt, Richard, and Mason, Tony, *Sport in Britain Since 1945* (Wiley-Blackwell, 2000)

Hyland, Francis P.M., *History of Galway Races* (Robert Hale Ltd, 2008)

Johnston Michael, *The Big Pot: The Story of the Irish Senior Rowing Championship 1912–1991* (Shandon Books, 1992)

Martin, John, *Ger McKenna on Greyhounds* (Interpet Publishing, 1989)

McBride, Willie John, and Bills, Peter, *Willie John: The Story of My Life* (Piatkus Books, 2004)

McDonnell, Frank, *The Story of Rushbrooke Lawn Tennis and Croquet Club: 1870–2007*, edited by Dan O'Regan (Rushbrooke, 2007)

Norridge, Julian, *Can We Have Our Balls Back, Please? How the British Invented Sport (And Then Almost Forgot How to Play It)* (Penguin, 2009)

O'Connell, Mick, *A Kerry Footballer* (Mercier Press, 1974)

O'Flynn, Diarmuid, *Hurling: The Warrior Game* (Penguin, 2008)

O'Hara, Denis, *The Remarkable Kyles* (O'Hara Publications, 2006)

O'Neill, Peter, and Boyne, Sean, *The Master of Doninga: The Authorised Biography of Paddy Mullins* (Mainstream Publishing, 1995)

Onslow, Richard, *The Heath and the Turf: A History of Newmarket* (Arthur Barker, 1971)

O'Sullivan, Sonia, with Tom Humphries, *Sonia: My Story* (Penguin, 2009)

Slavin, Michael, *Showjumping Legends: Ireland 1868–1998* (Wolfhound Press, 1998)

Stanaland, Peggy, 'The Tailteann Games of Ancient Ireland: Their Origin, Growth and